CAPITAL

MARK HAGE

CAPITAL

A PUBLIC SPACE BOOKS

For the City of New York, infinite playground
of thought and blunder

What closes and then darkness,
what opens and then bright?
Before the horn has risen,
where hides the lord of light?

—TIAN WEN,
A CHINESE BOOK OF ORIGINS

How you frame something is a moral decision.

—BABETTE MANGOLTE

Leave it the fuck alone.

—A PASSERBY

BROOM SWEPT

On Mercer Street, on the island of Manhattan, and just before the city paused, walking in a southerly direction from Houston to Canal, there was a decimation. A Chicxulub to mercantilism. Even then, in prophetic unease, the stores had shuttered in blatant proportions, without much replacement or activity. Upped and gone together: the high-mark Italian brand, the chain retailer, the individual who borrowed from parent and friend with dreams of a place in the pantheon of commerce.

This was not restricted to SoHo or the other high-rent districts. It was also the small enterprise on the side street: tailor and small baker, laundromat and diner, deli and shoe repairer. Signs taped to doors thanked patrons for the years, or more dubious signs claimed temporary closure due to flooding, a return after summer vacation or—masked with brown paper—improvements to come. Small larcenies now absorbed into the wider calamity.

The reverse direction of occupancy is decay. It has nothing ceremonial. No ribbon cutting or fresh flowers, no eager attendants. Empty, the precious architectural image relaxes into anti-heroic and shabby availability. But there is a scale of concern. In prior days, on its own, an empty store evoked a light curiosity and anticipation for its future. At a larger frequency of closures, there is a different kind of memory at play, closer to dread than nostalgia, a bereavement for a city rapidly becoming something else.

I walked the city, intent on documenting retail stores that had failed or closed, existing in an amalgamation of abandoned objects, archaeologies, and recent interventions. The gouge next to the mastic that had held a mirror, mysterious interim brush-strokes, the re-emerging ferrous column cast in sand moulds. An Arte Povera of sorts decided away from the professional class.

A space while in use exists in the constraint of intention. Specific and close to tyrannical in the way it is experienced, it supersedes the conflicting remains of the accumulated past. But with time, these times, through surrender or exhaustion, the space becomes a hasty victim itself. Tools tear at its obsolescence, revealing its layers. Permanence and absence, ruins and remnants.

These resulting patterns, these accidents, reveal a conglomerate. At first, the tenants who leave behind what they see of no value or, with hope for their deposit back, manage lease-mandated laundered spaces. In their aftermath, those who act on behalf of the landlord arrive. They make remodeling decisions based on what appeals to climate and prospective tenant, but with minimal expenditure. They hang a For Rent sign, and with no plans or sketches, order a few workers by waving their hands. The last party to this congress are the demolition workers. They nod, barely listen and demolish what they think should go, spare what they think should stay, mostly based on simple precautions and the difficulty or ease of their task.

Walking the city, I found myself drawn to these spaces as a refuge. Weary of the guarantees of perpetual design, an insistence that had saturated our lives and displaced meaning. Venturing out again, I find solace in these fleeting compositions that lack intent. Their sculptural logic and painterly rhythms, so at ease, which at some point, in the churn of our resumed ways, will never be seen again.

In these hybrid spaces, a spirit of labors comes through, anonymous labors that have come and gone, disparate hands that built the years, the same hands that built the city. In these worlds, there is ambiguity and hope, the emotion of aesthetic surprise. A return to a city we once knew. Our broom-swept Acropolis. The temporal majesty of scarred, wide-open ghosts.

—Mark Hage,
New York City, 2020

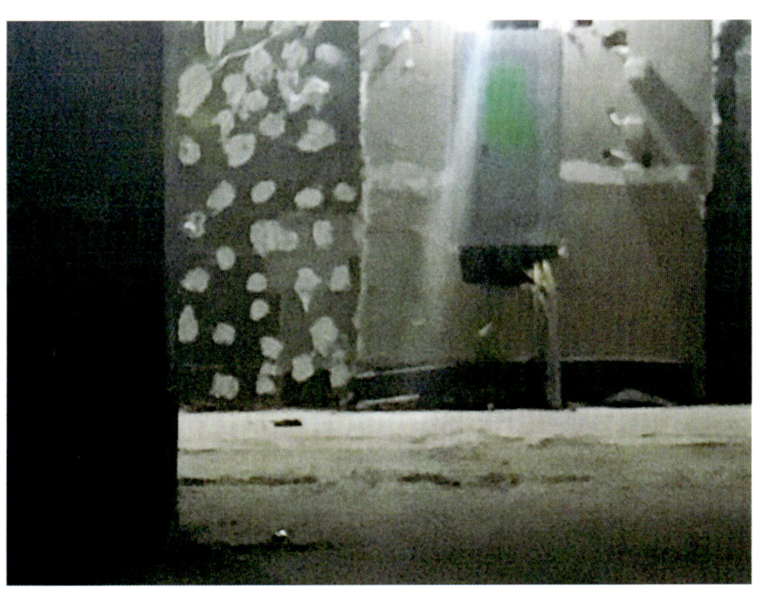

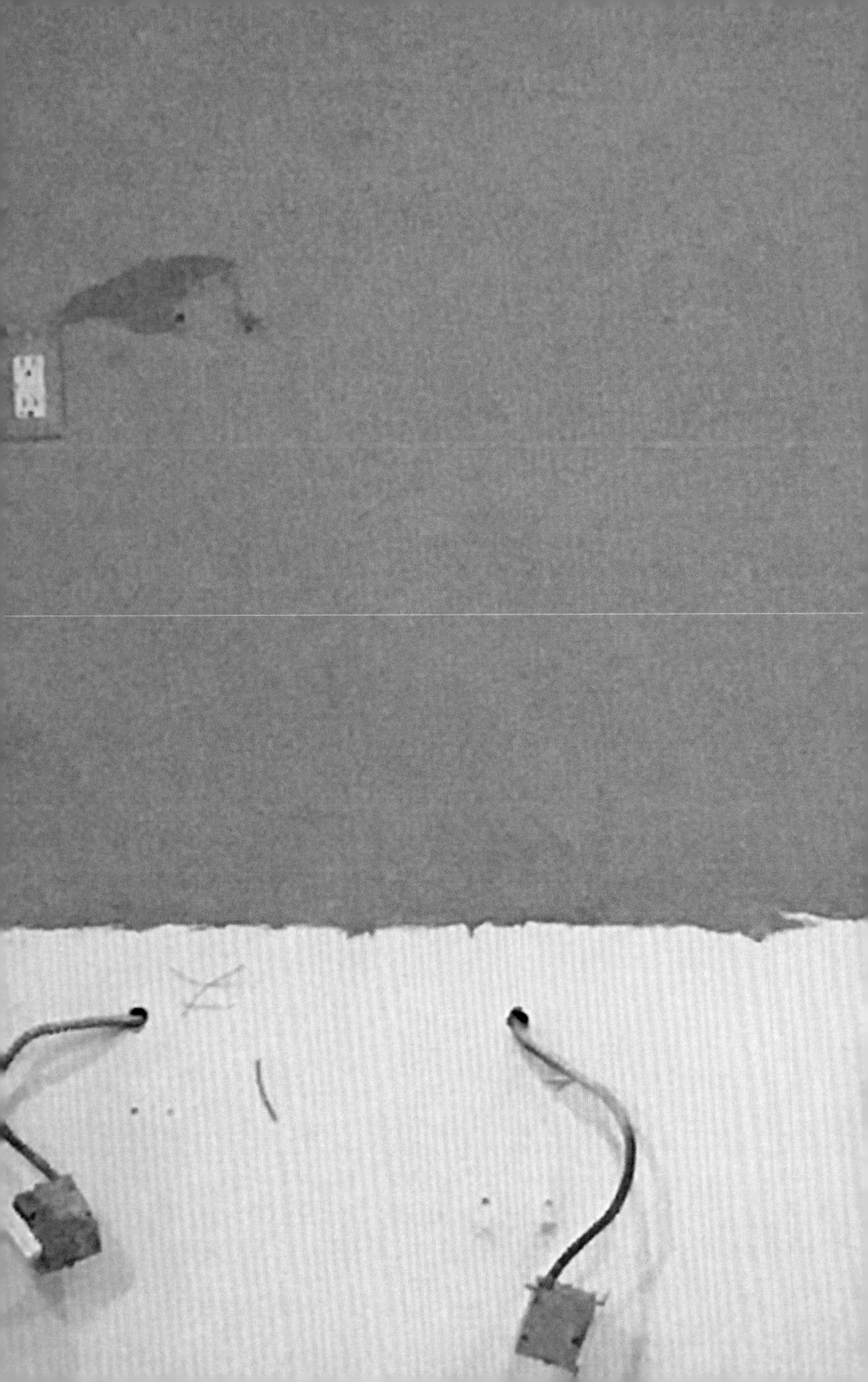

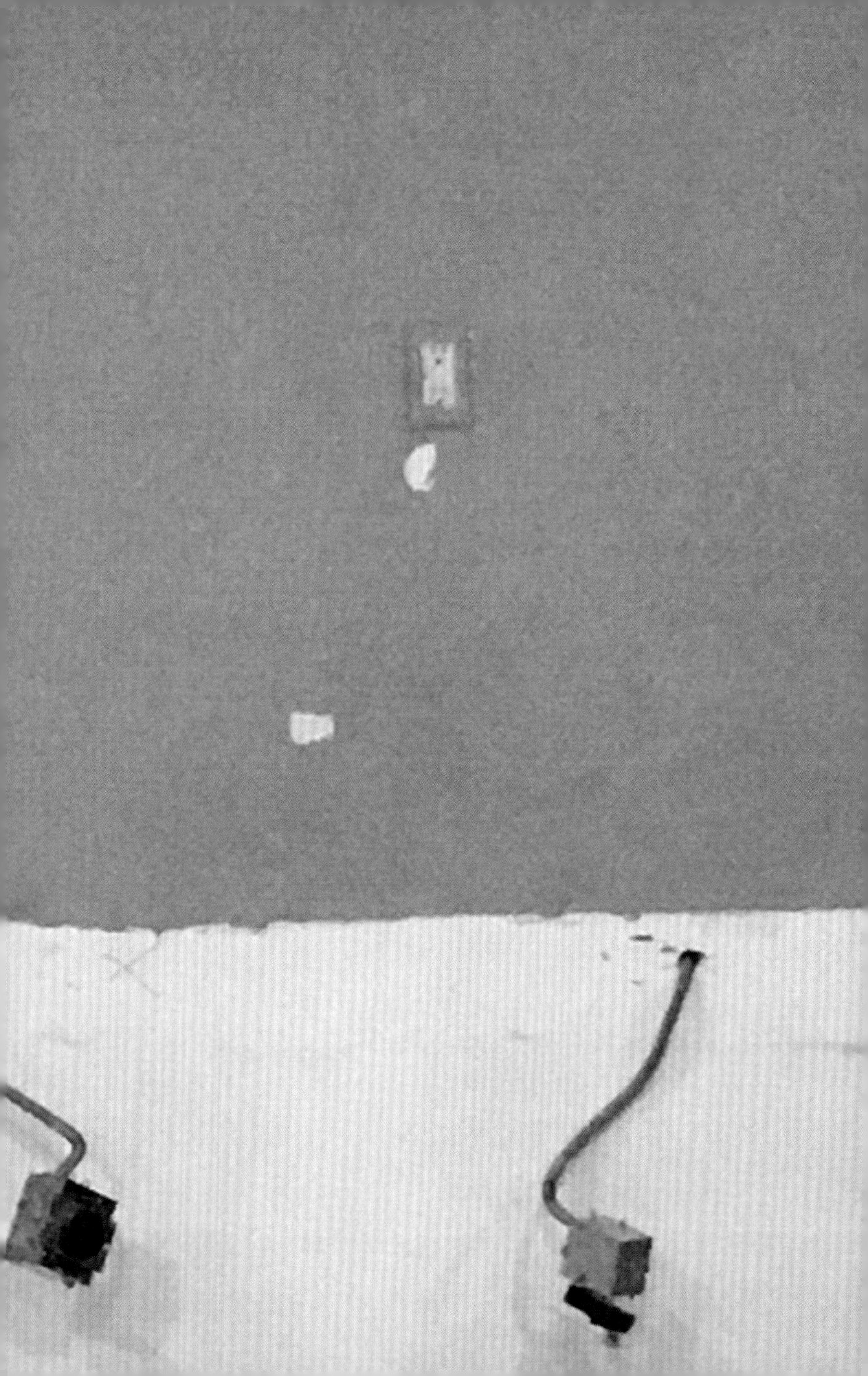

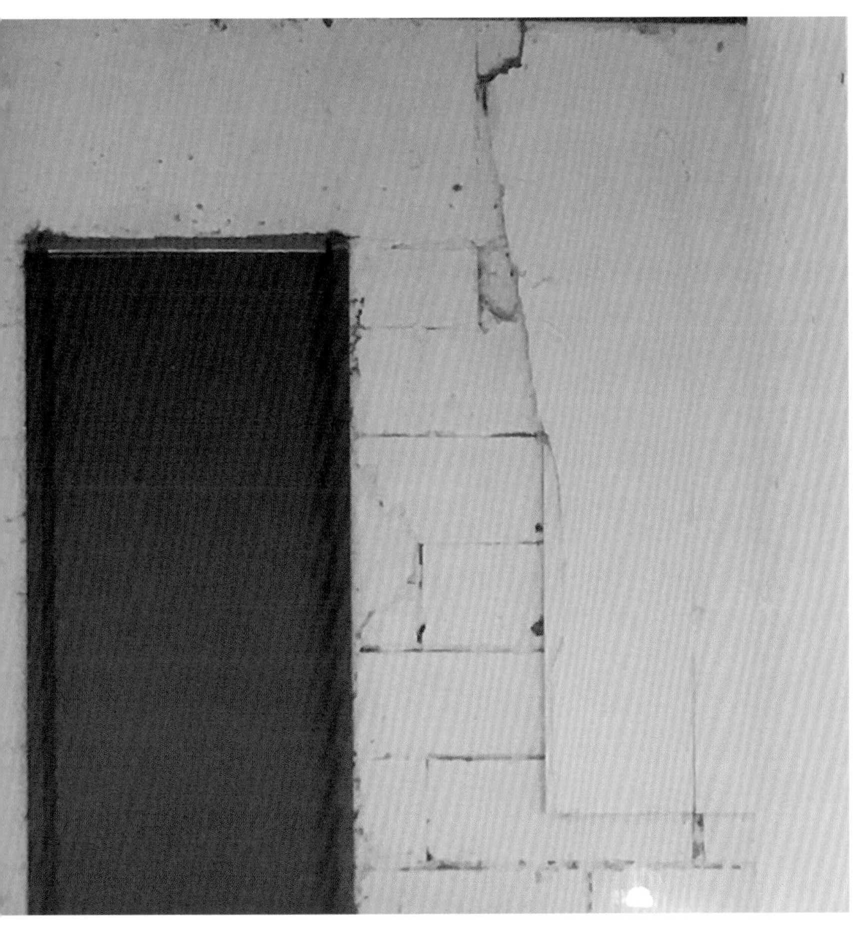

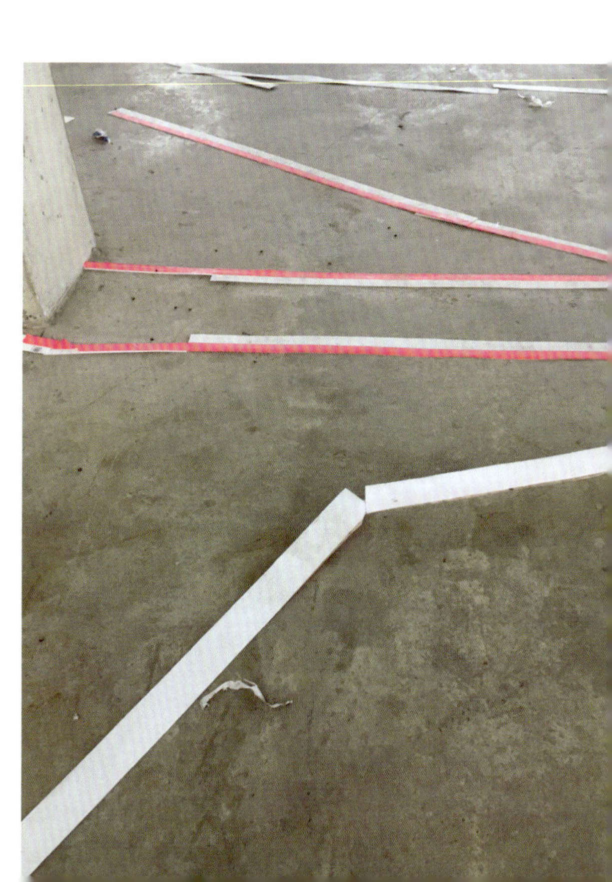

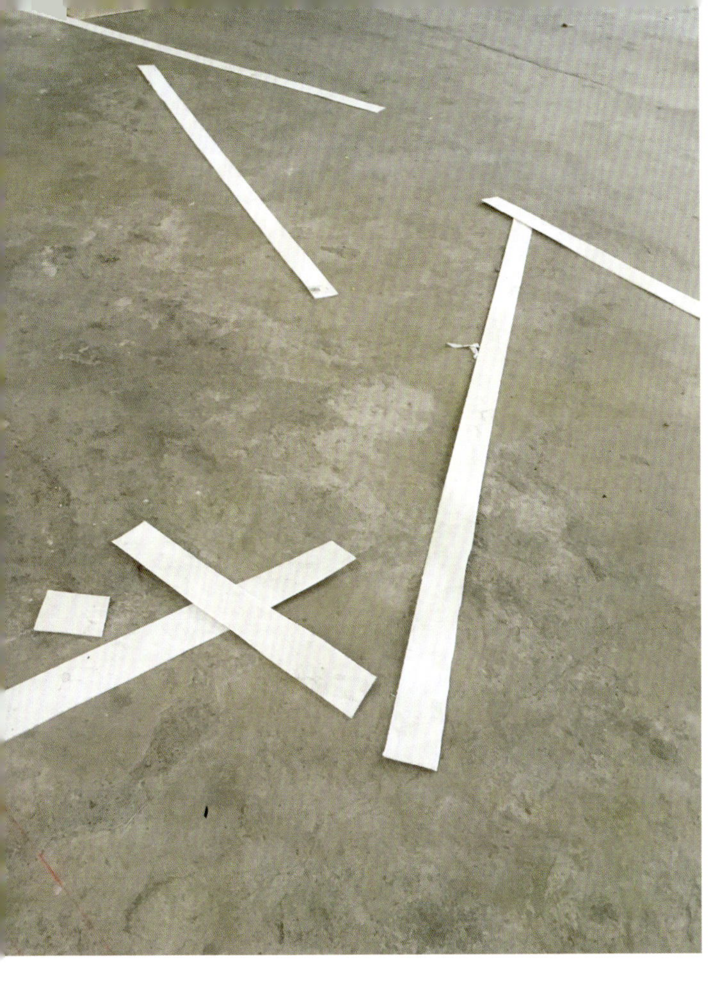

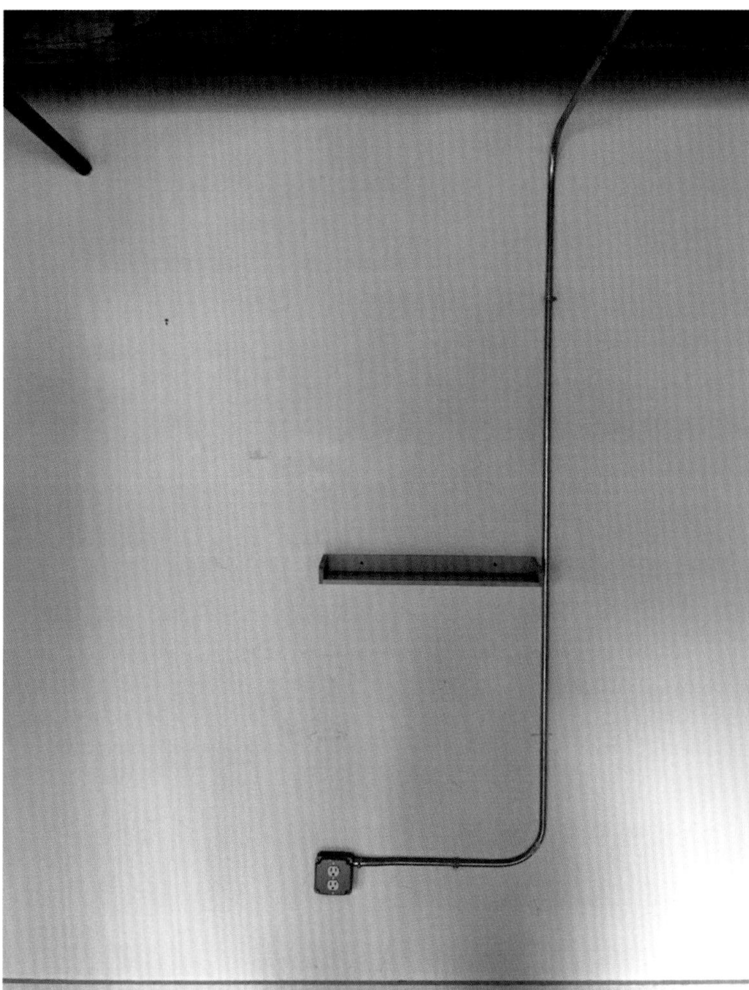

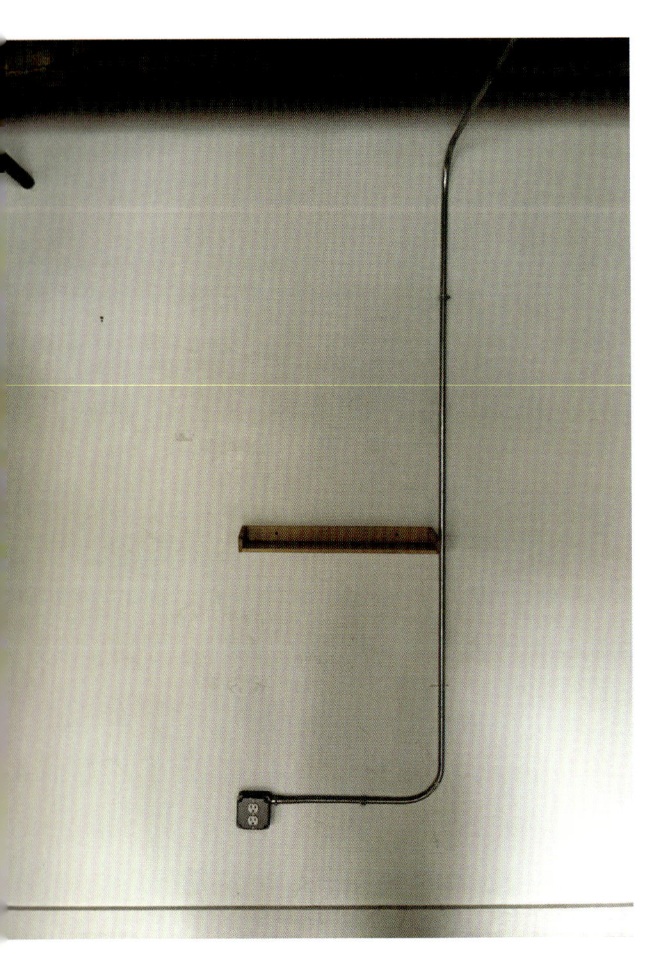

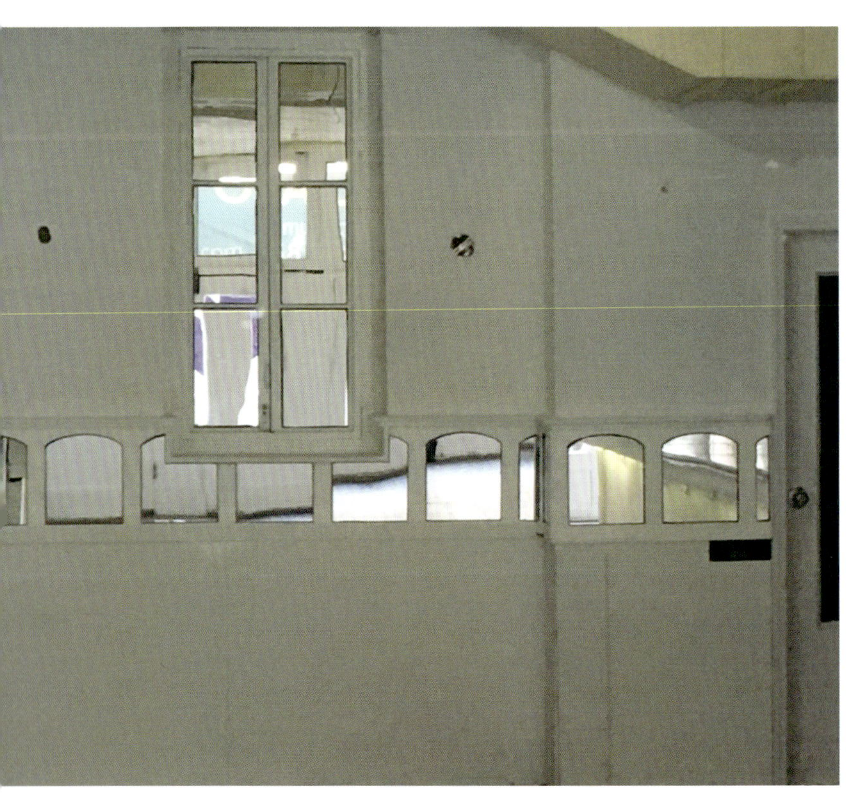

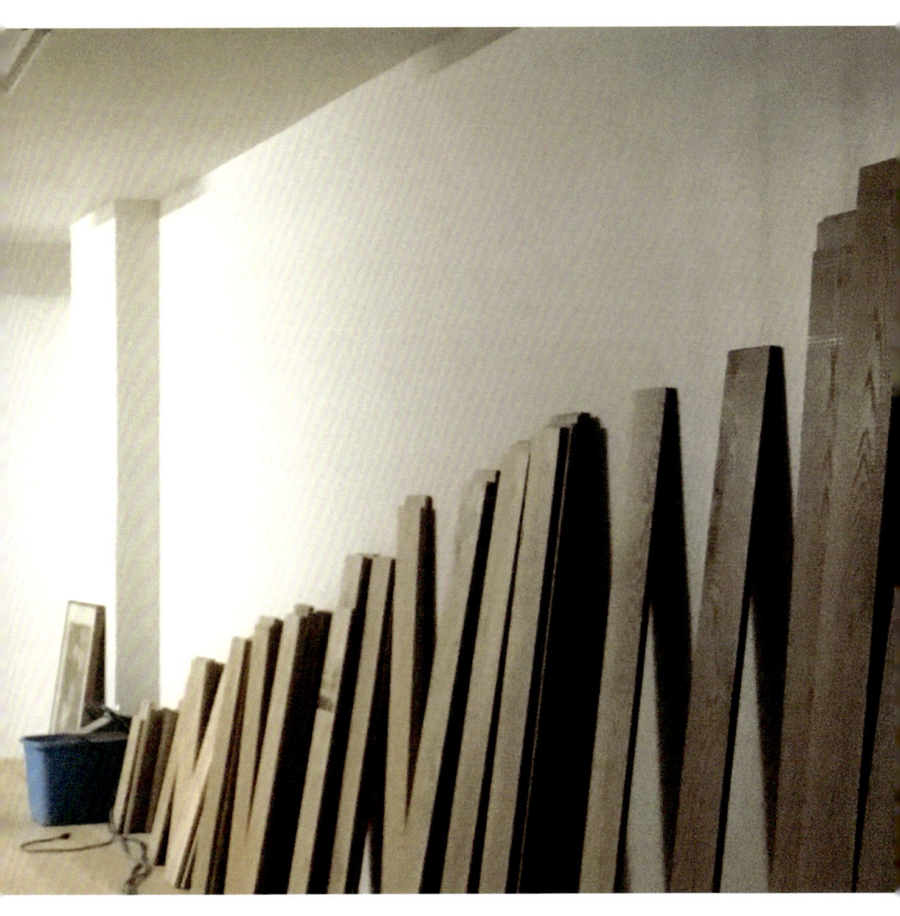

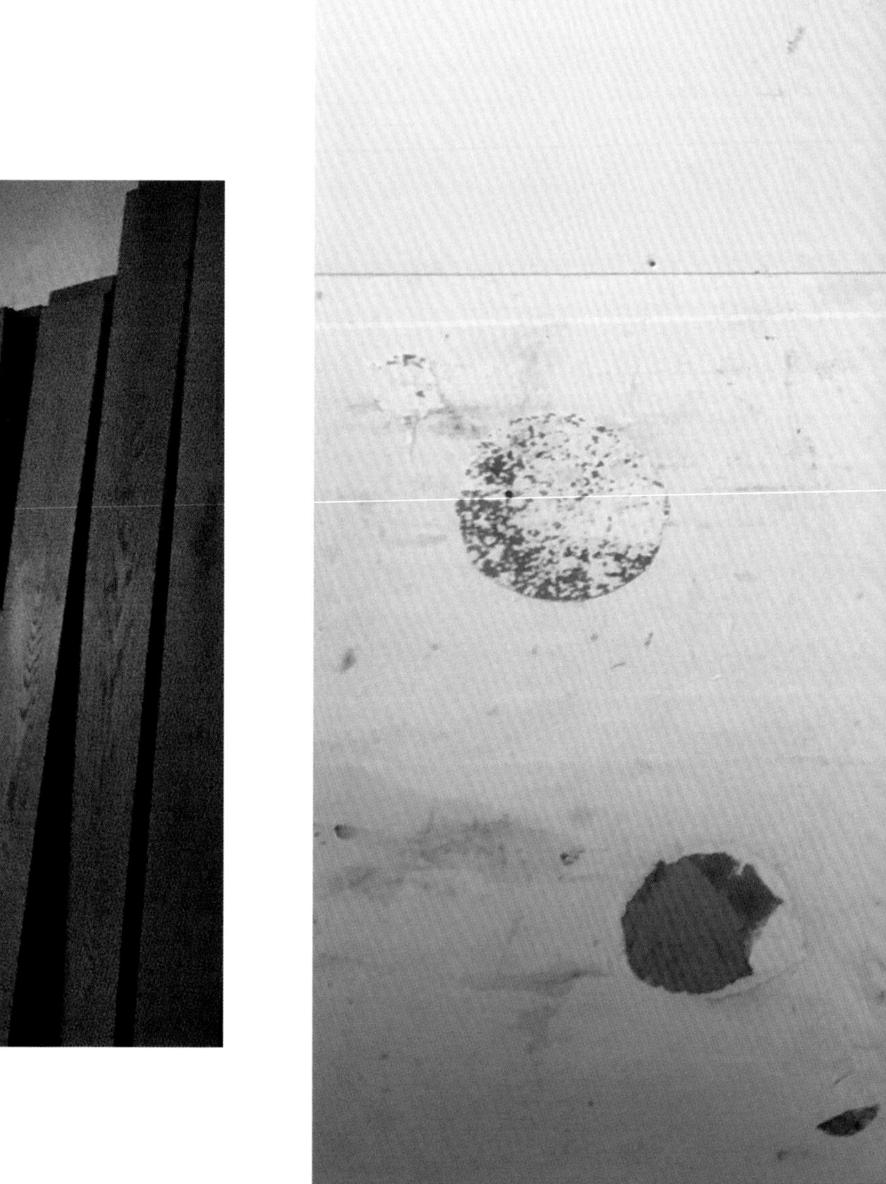

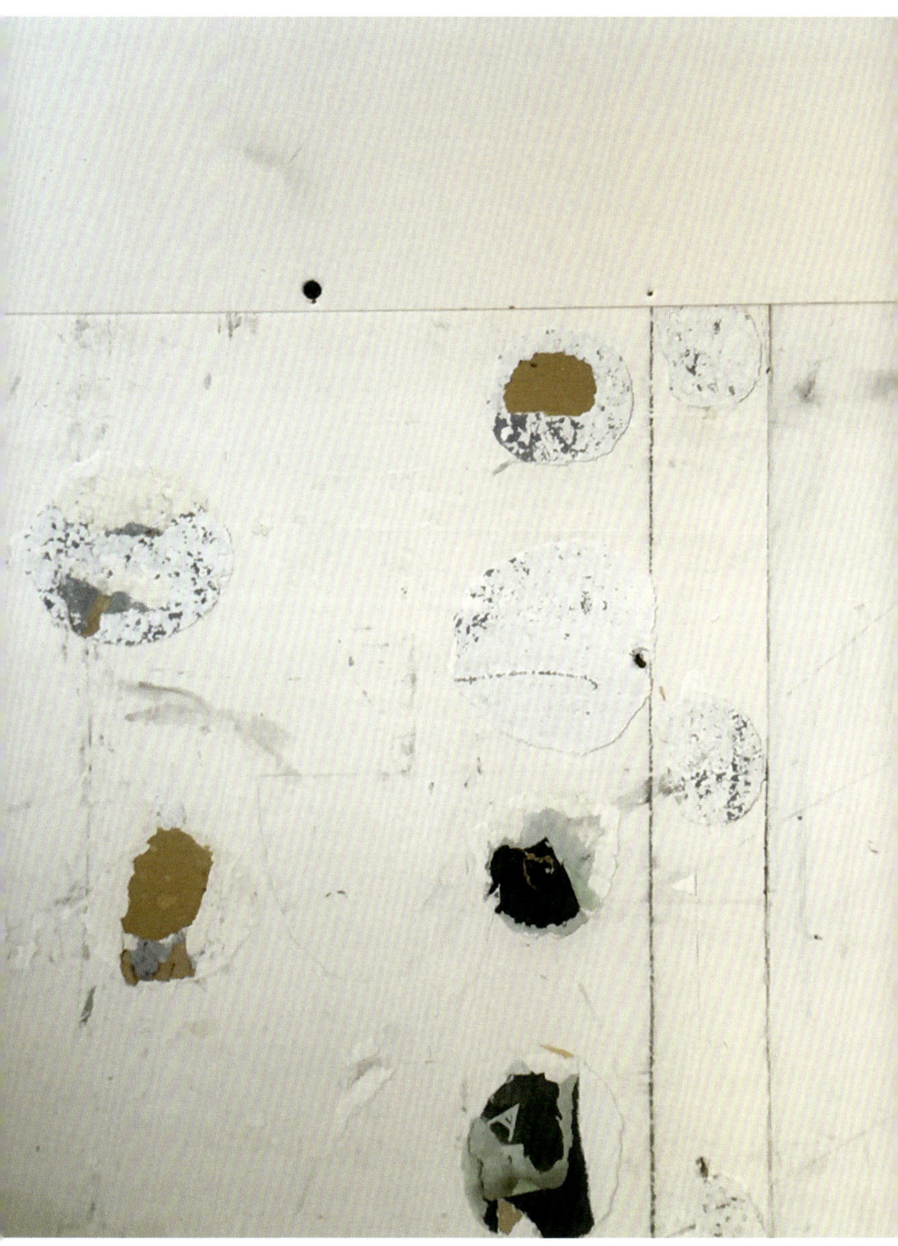

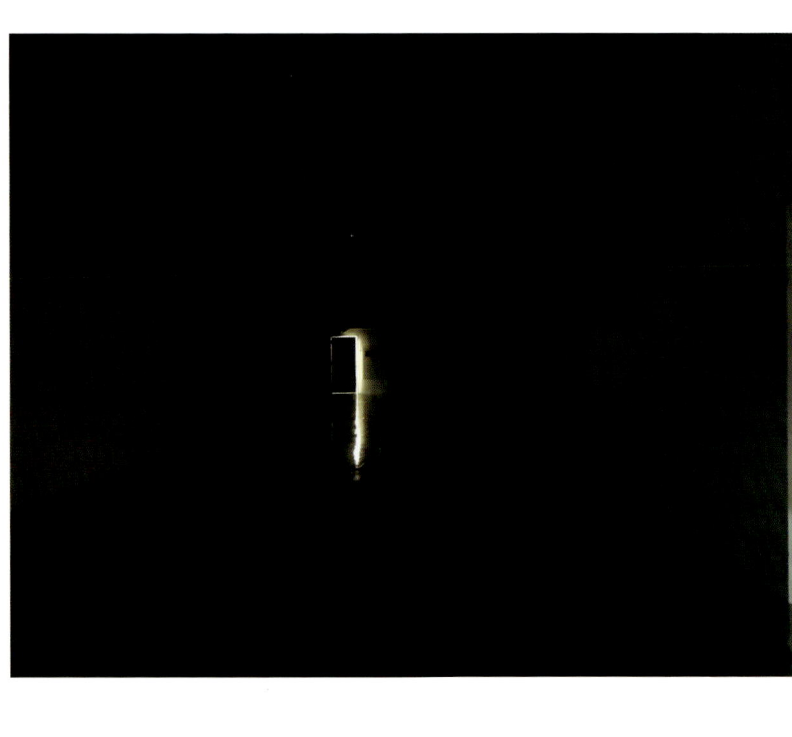

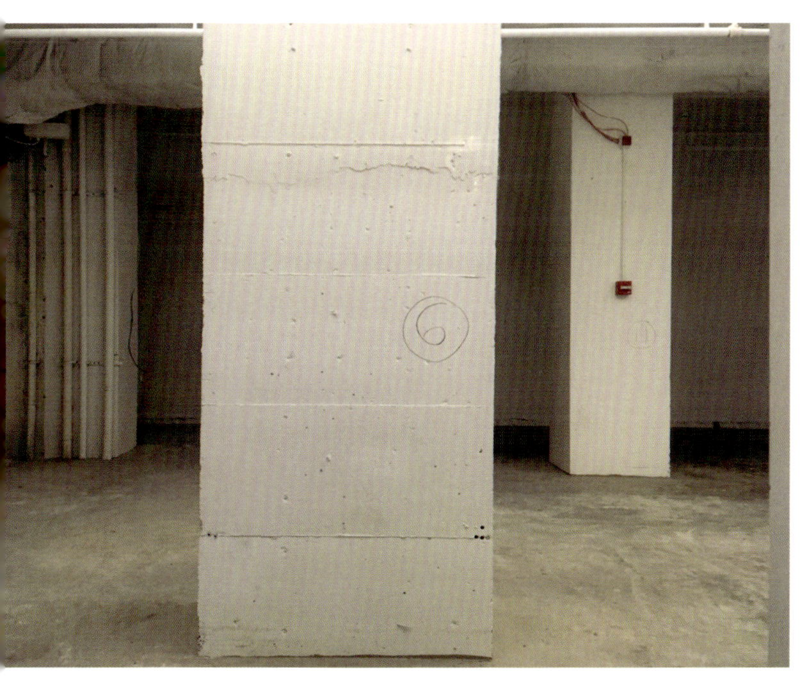
6

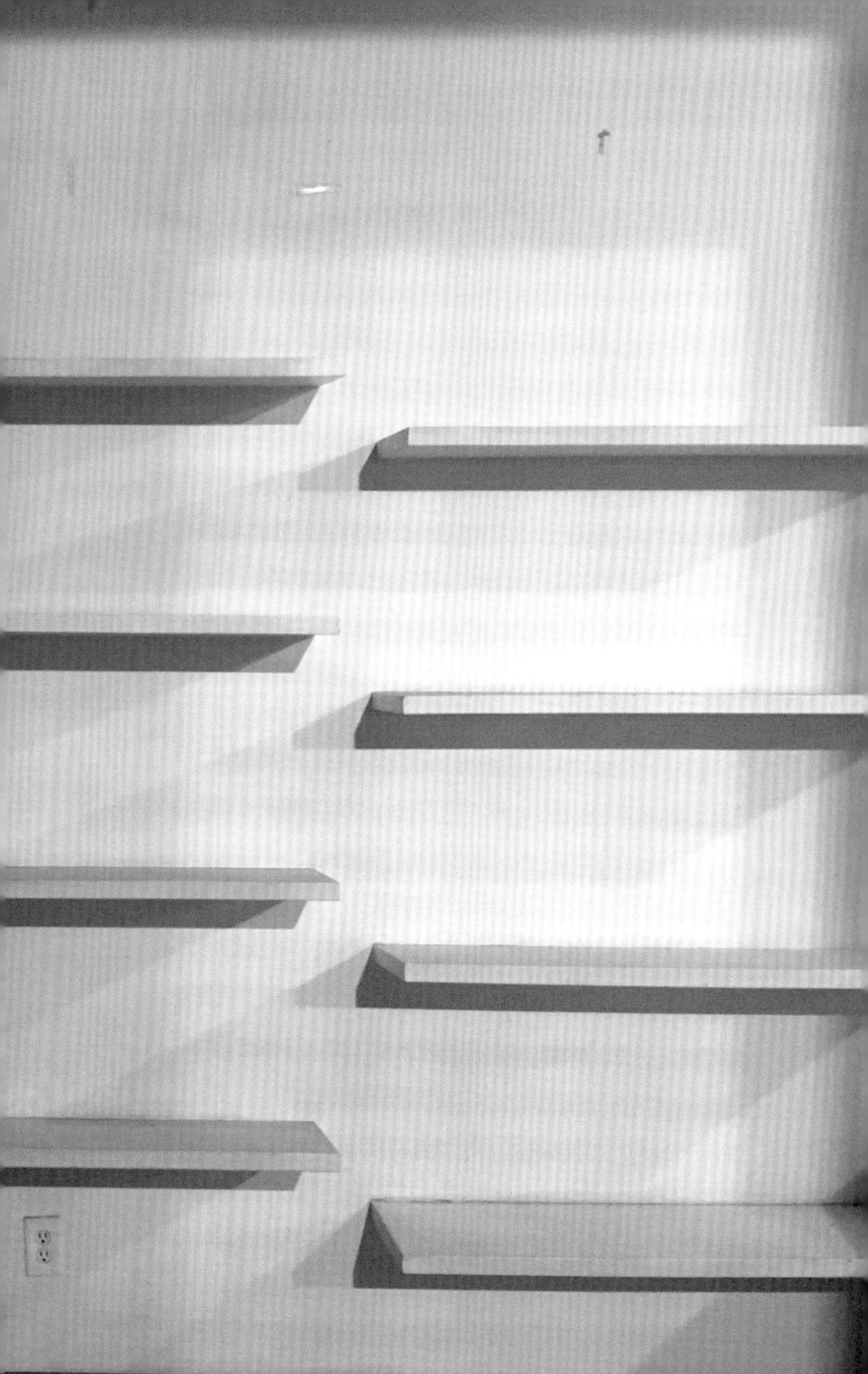

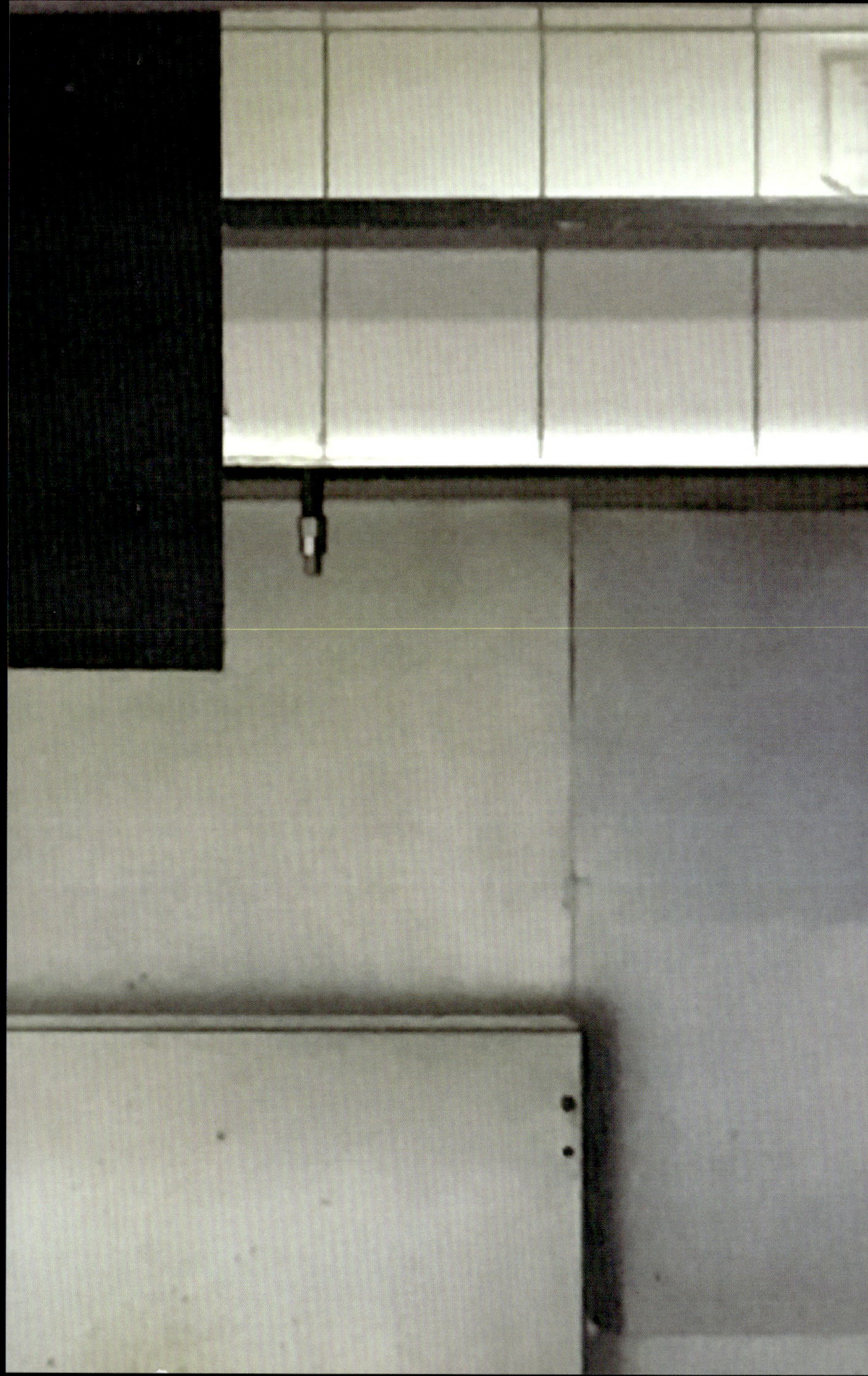

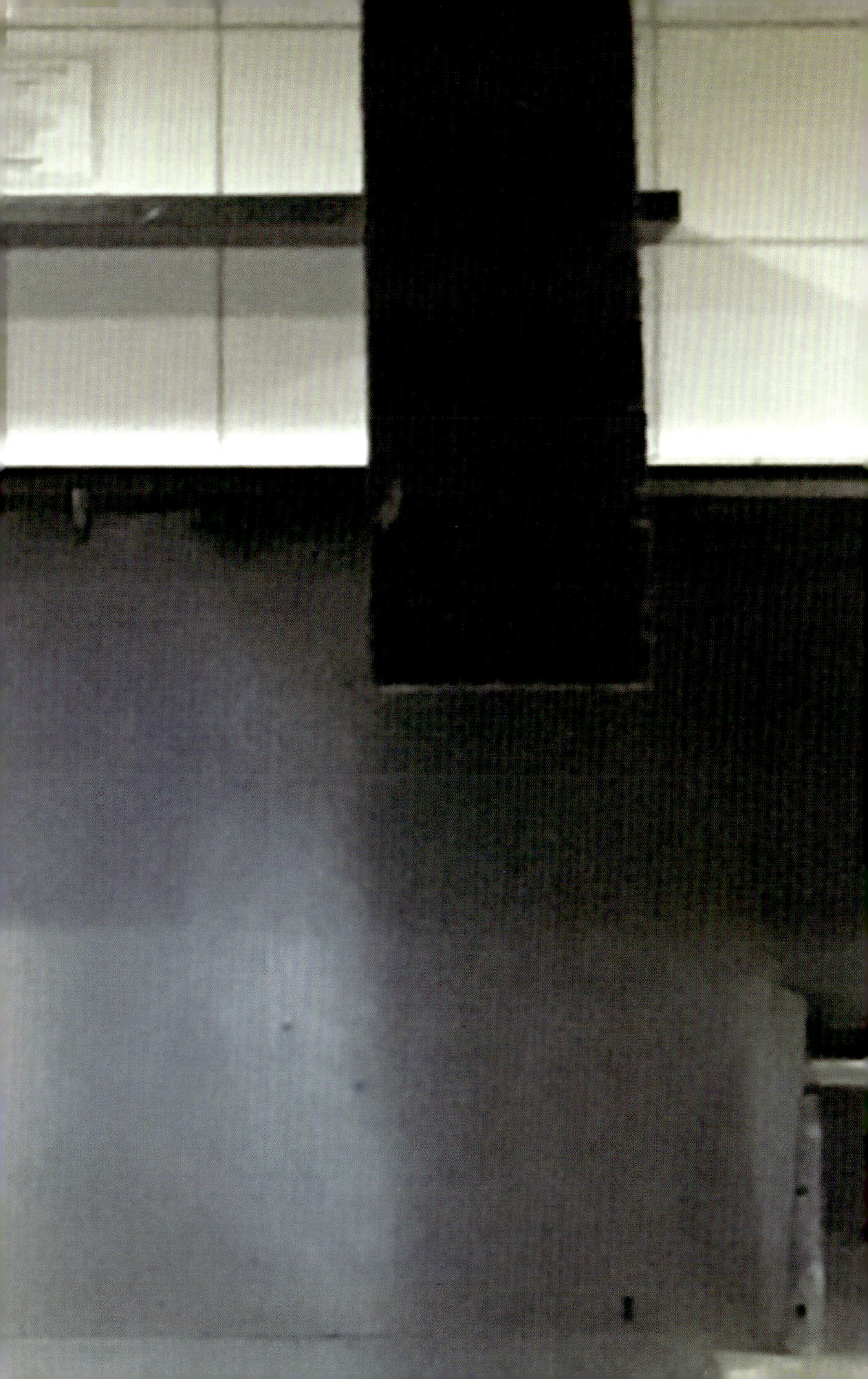

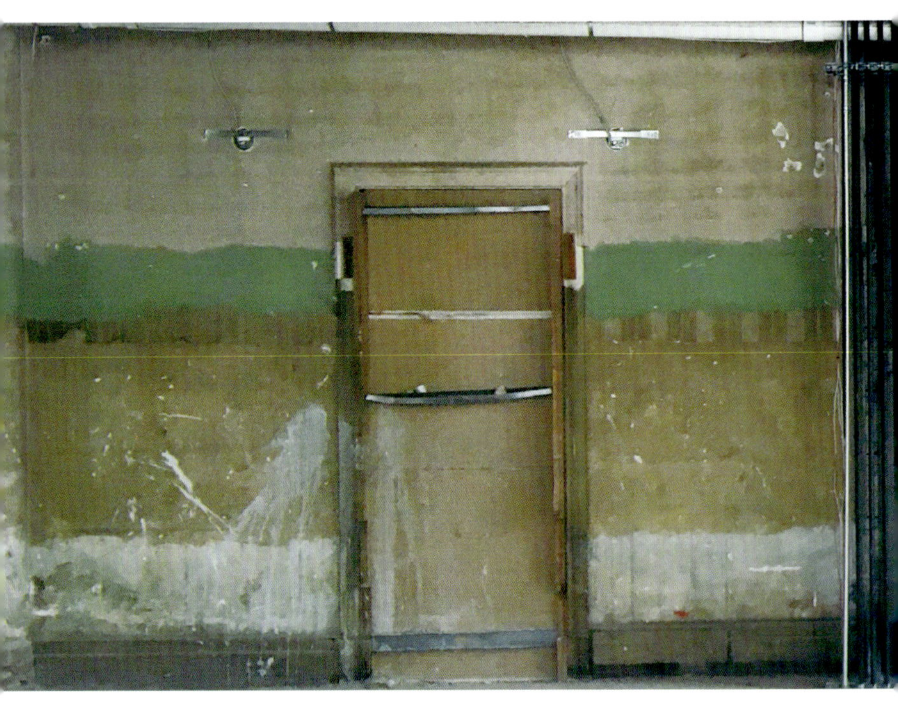

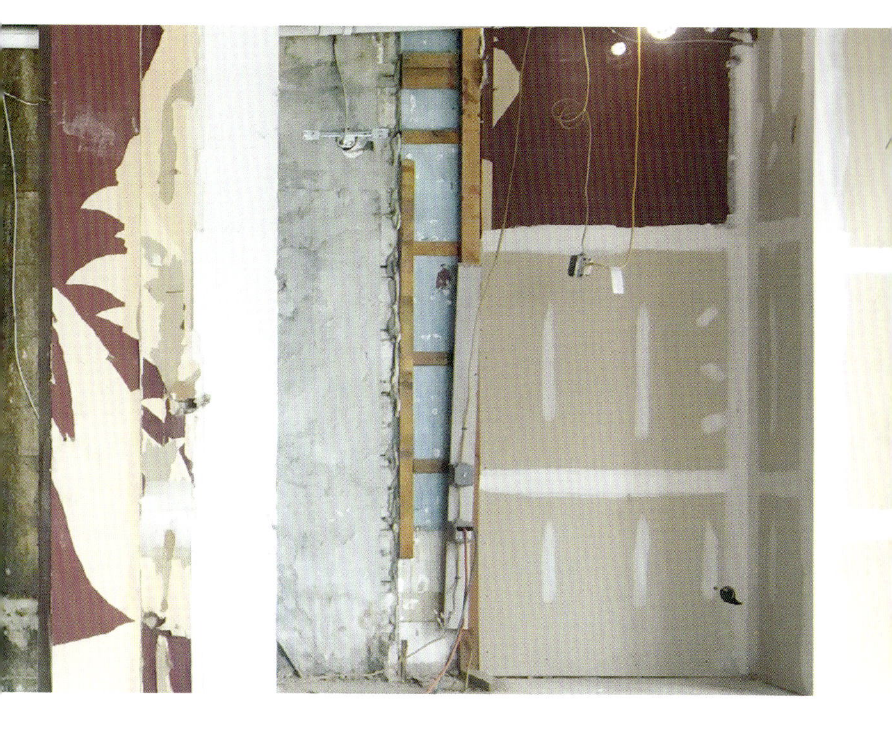

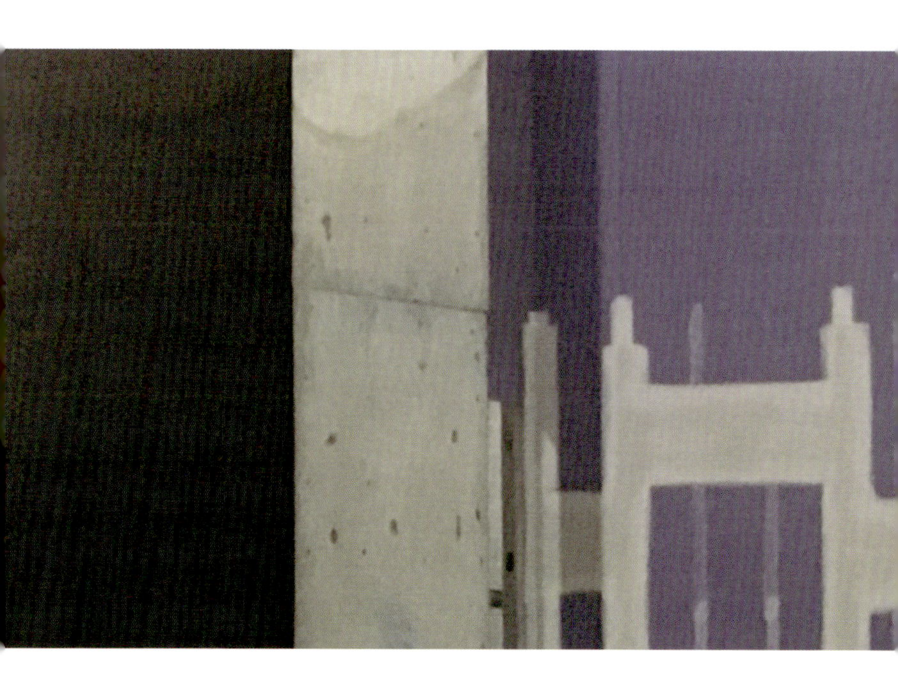

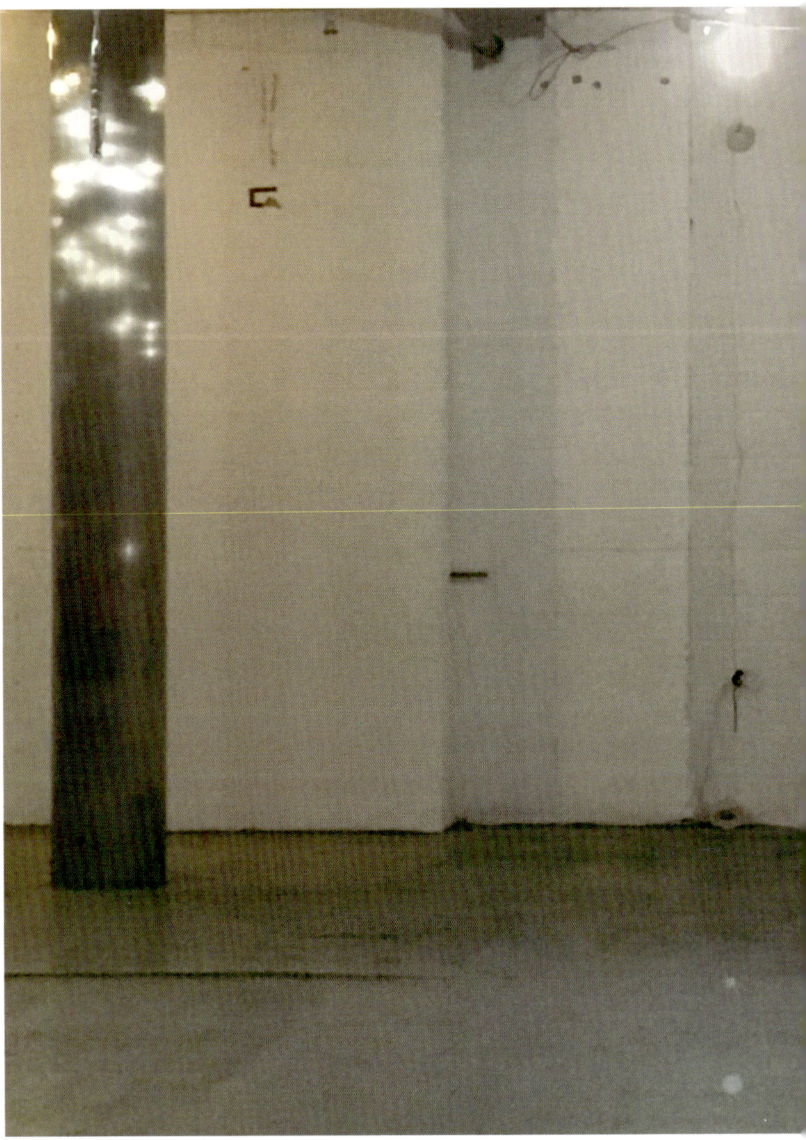

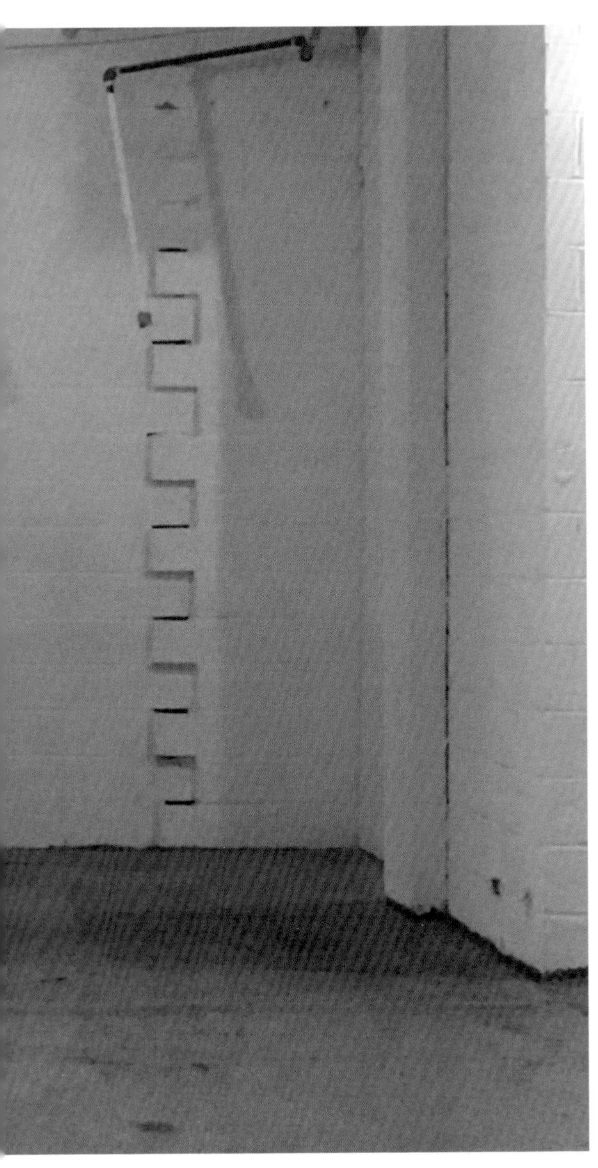

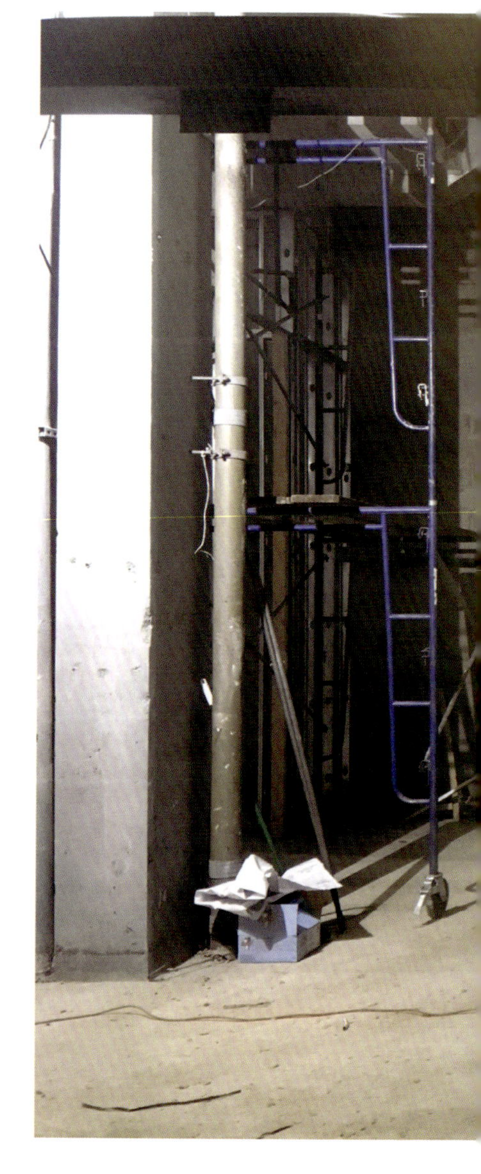

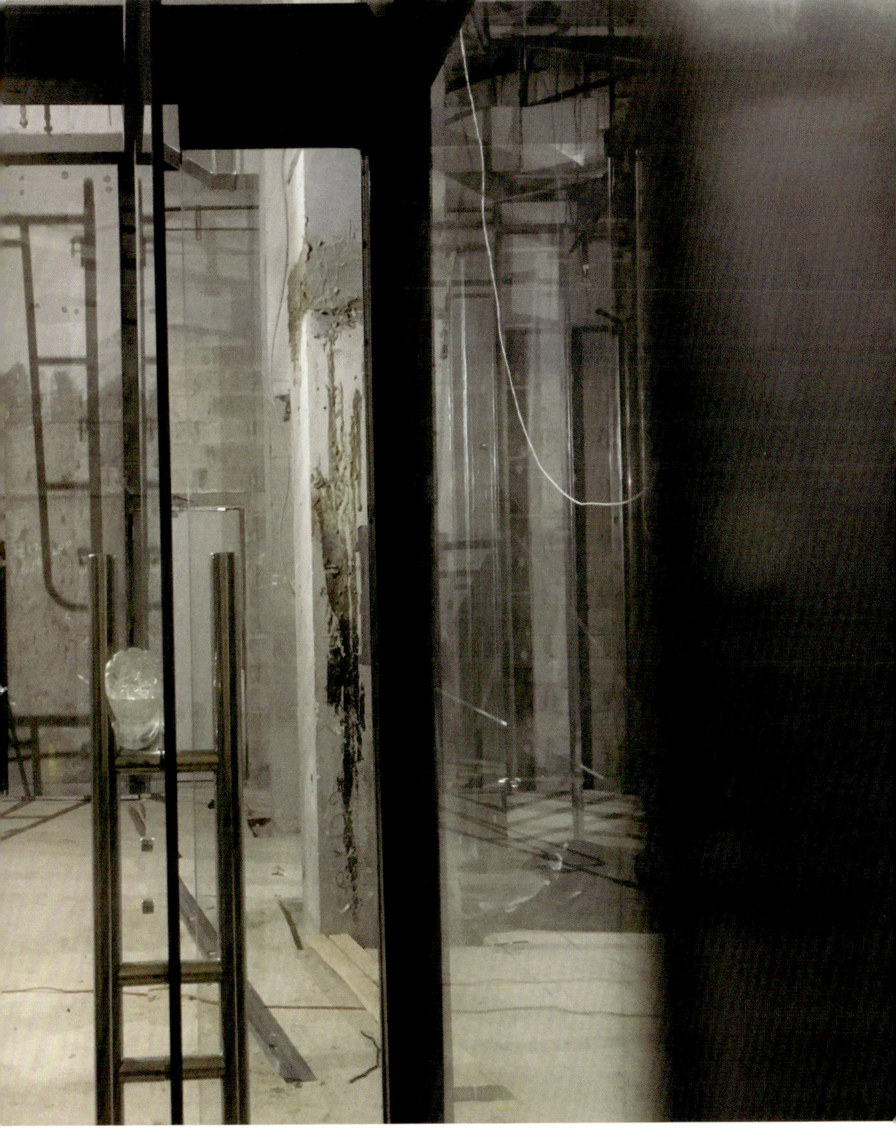

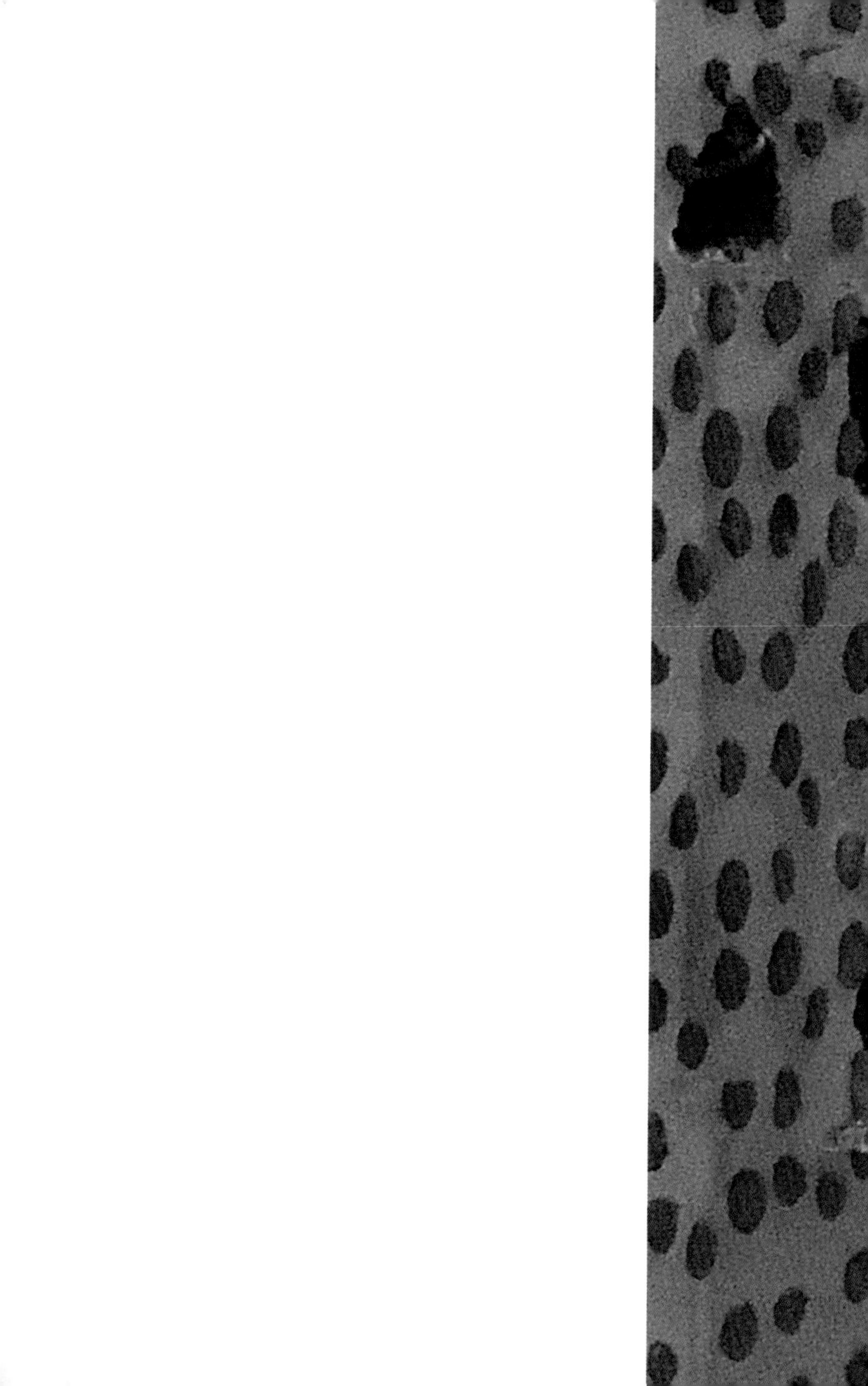

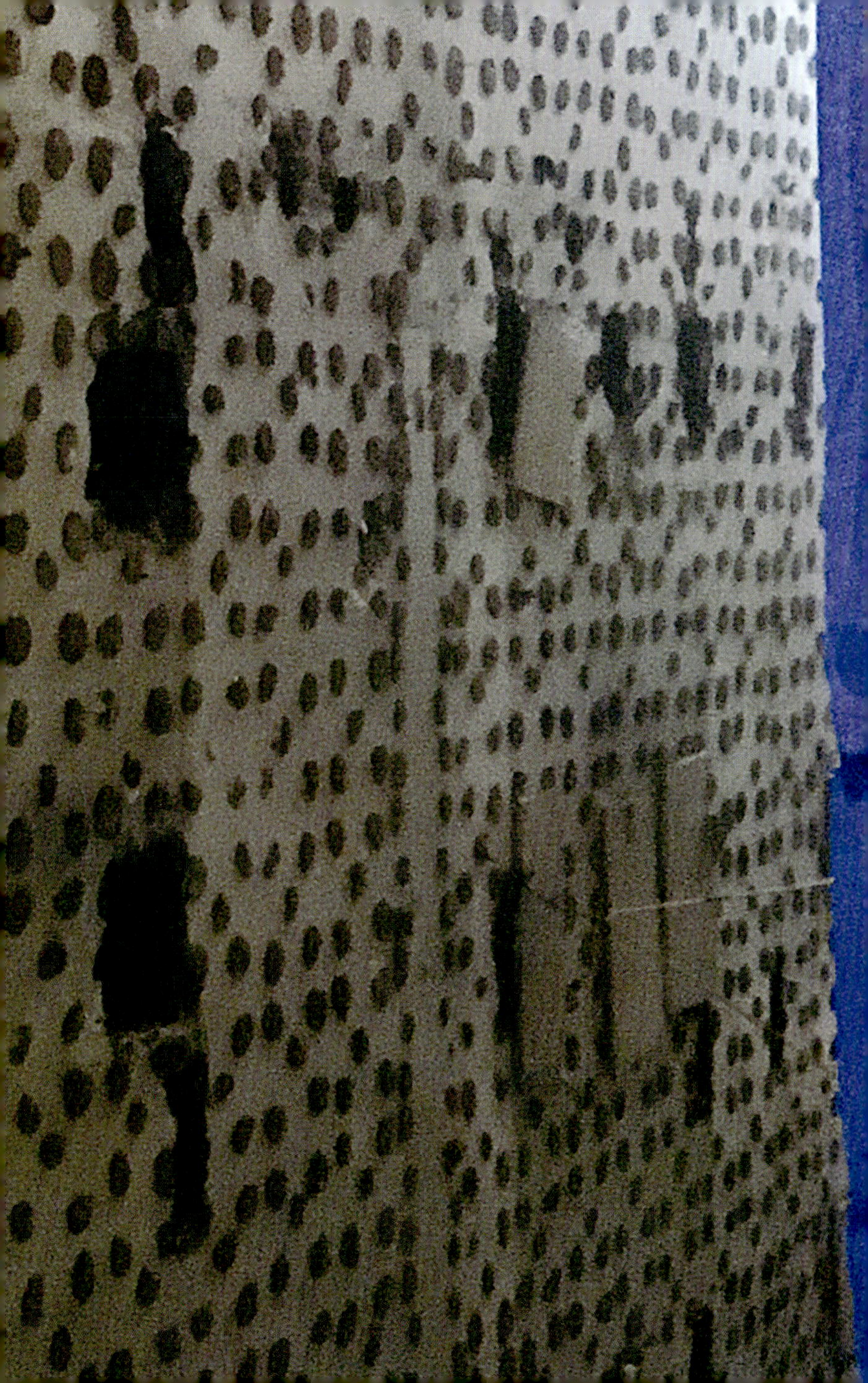

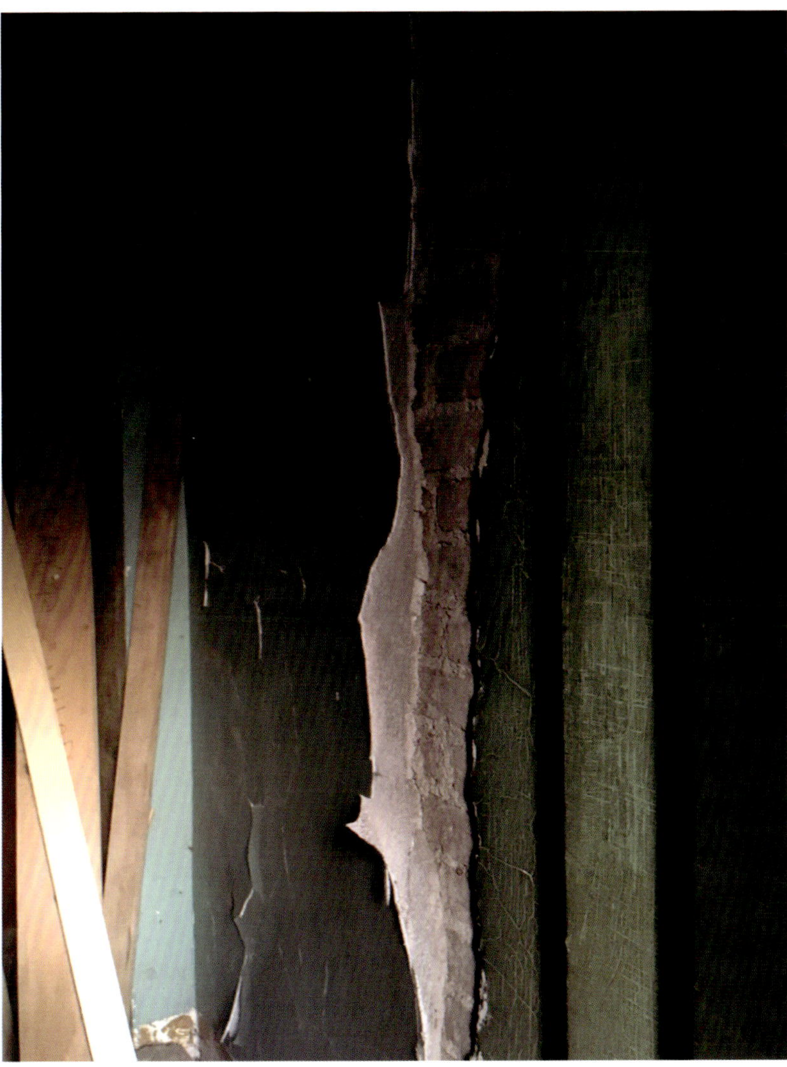

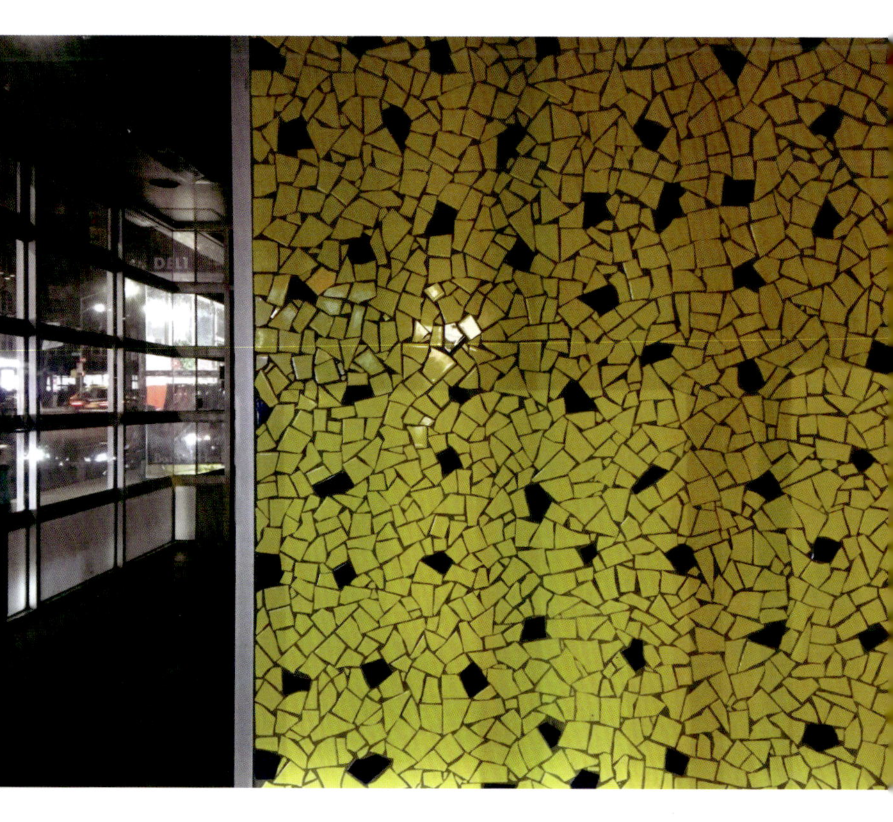
DELI

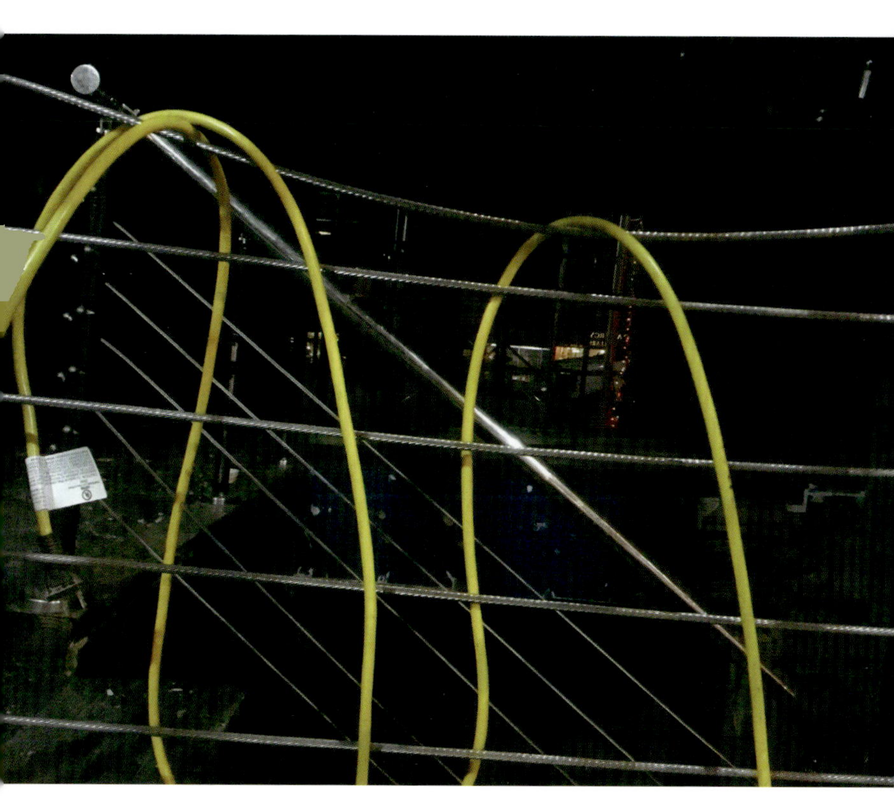

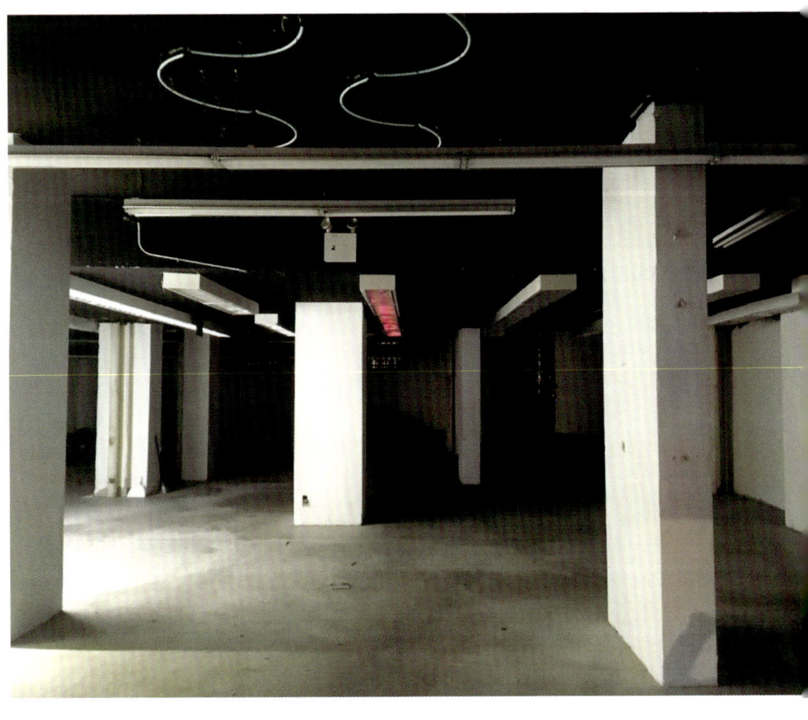

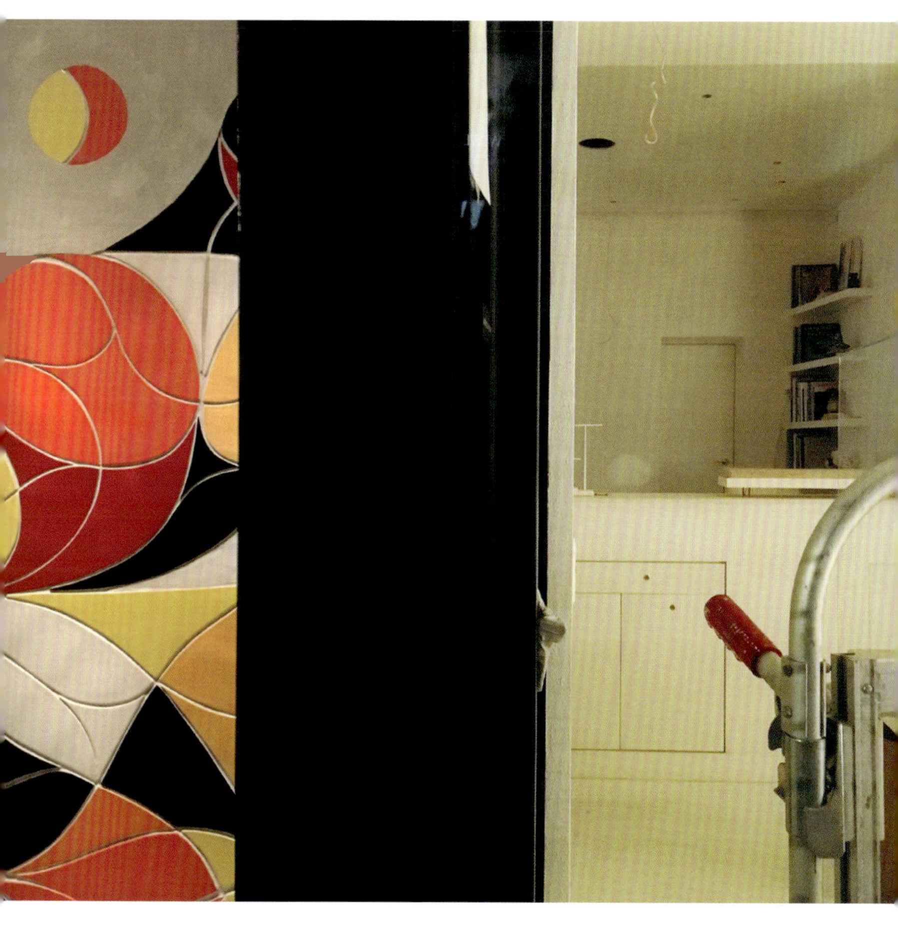

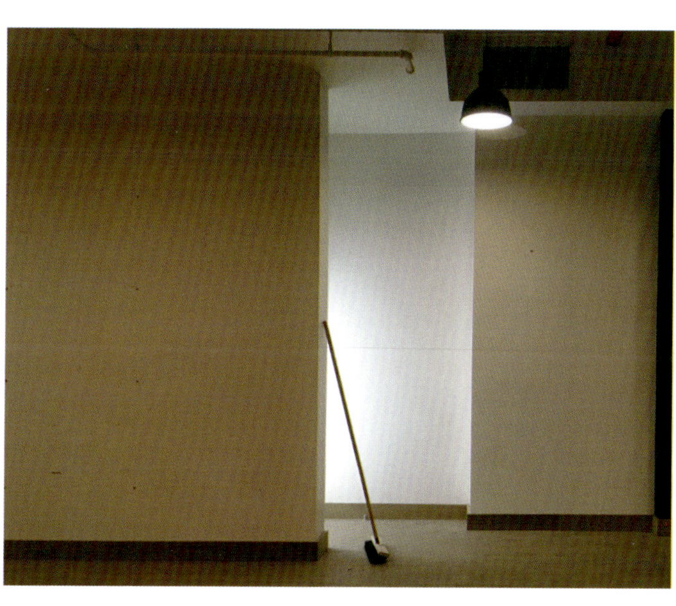

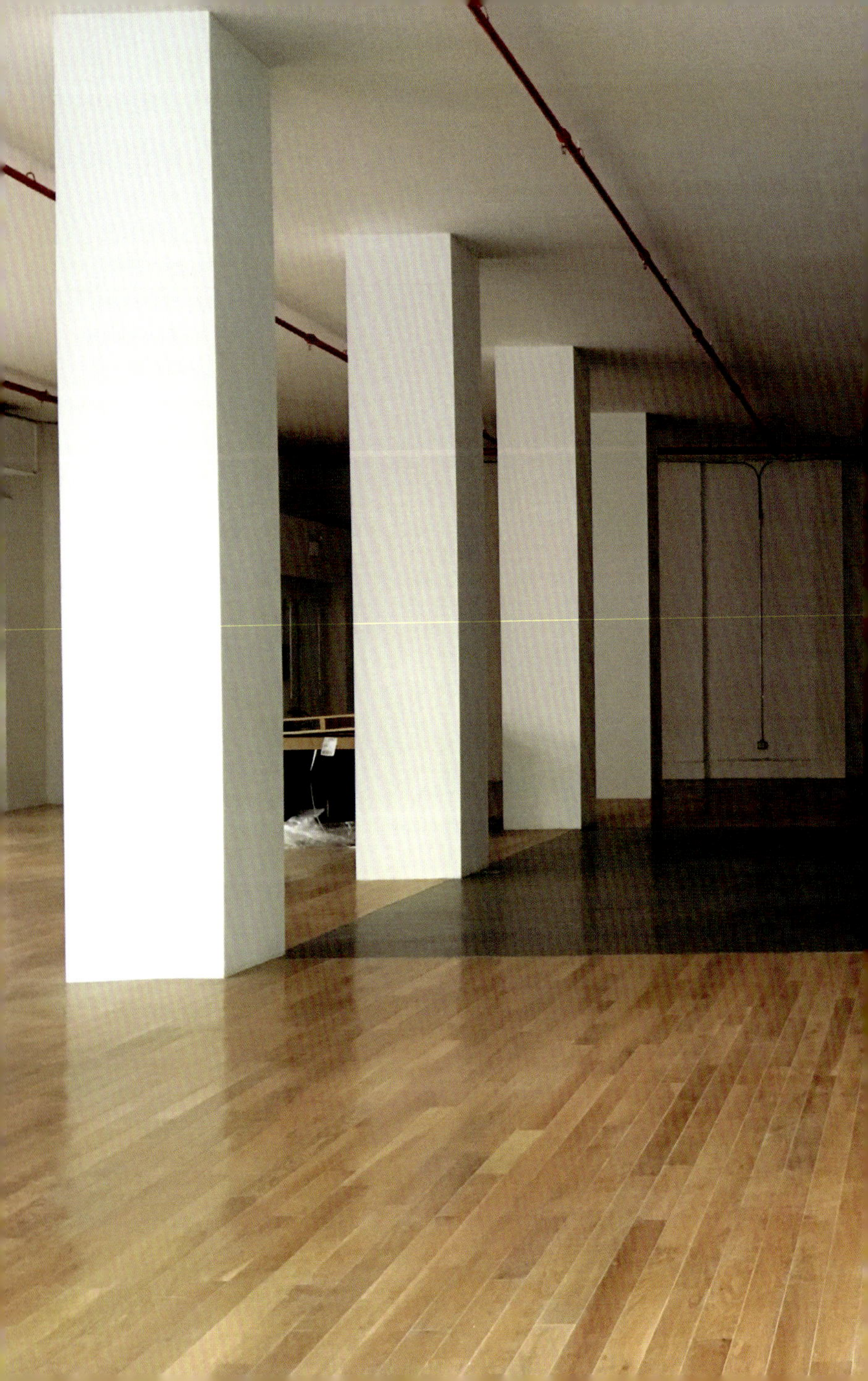

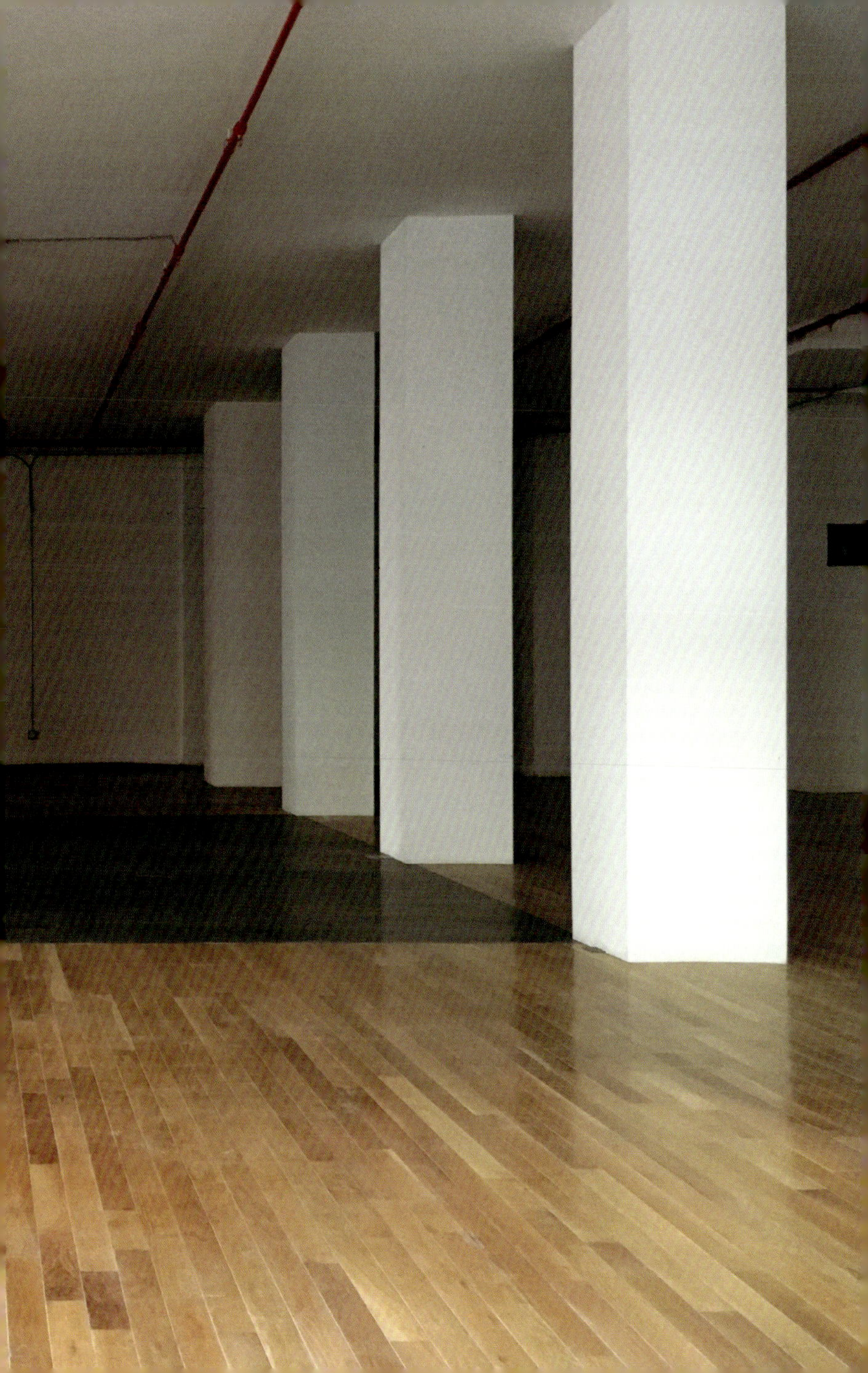

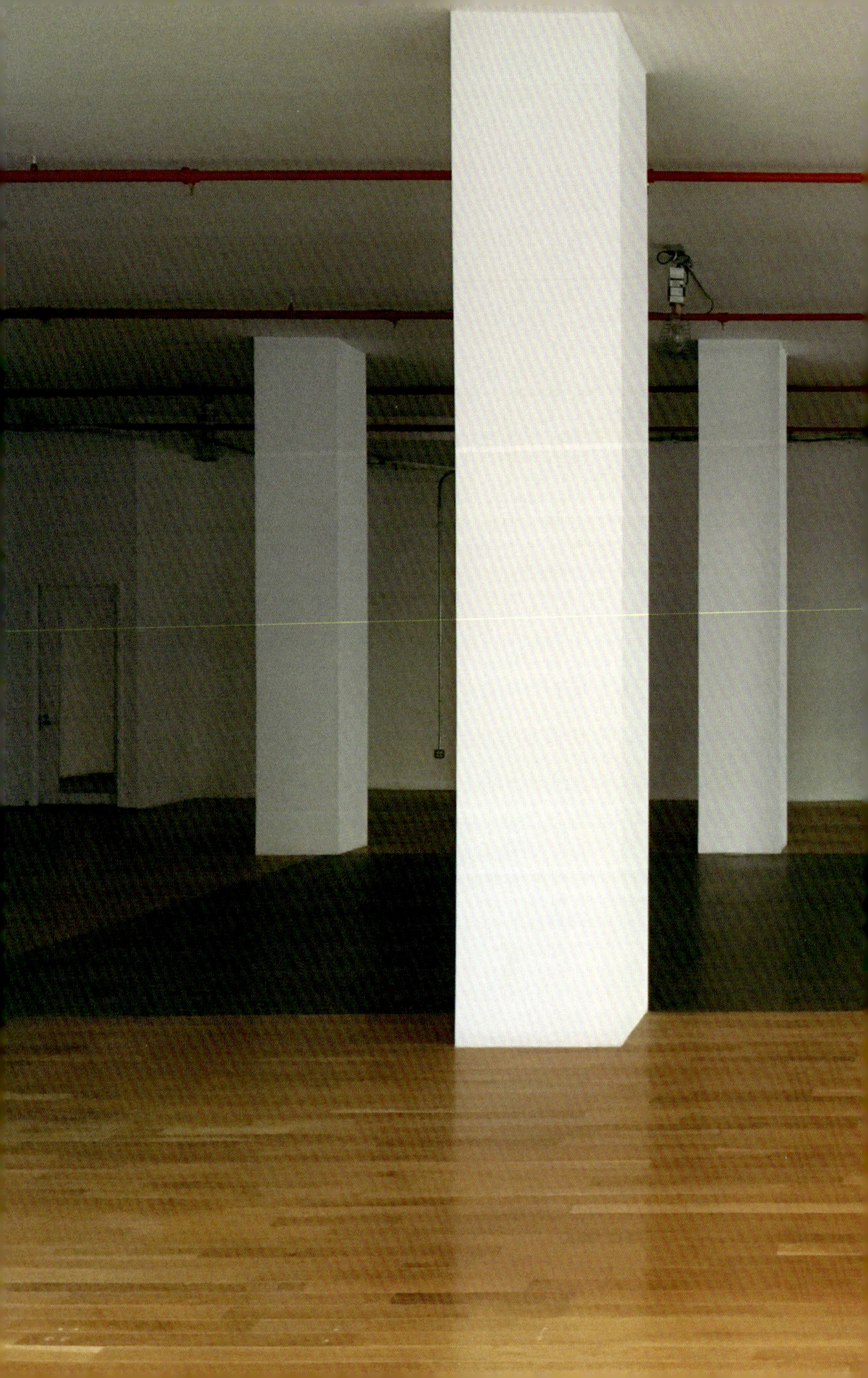

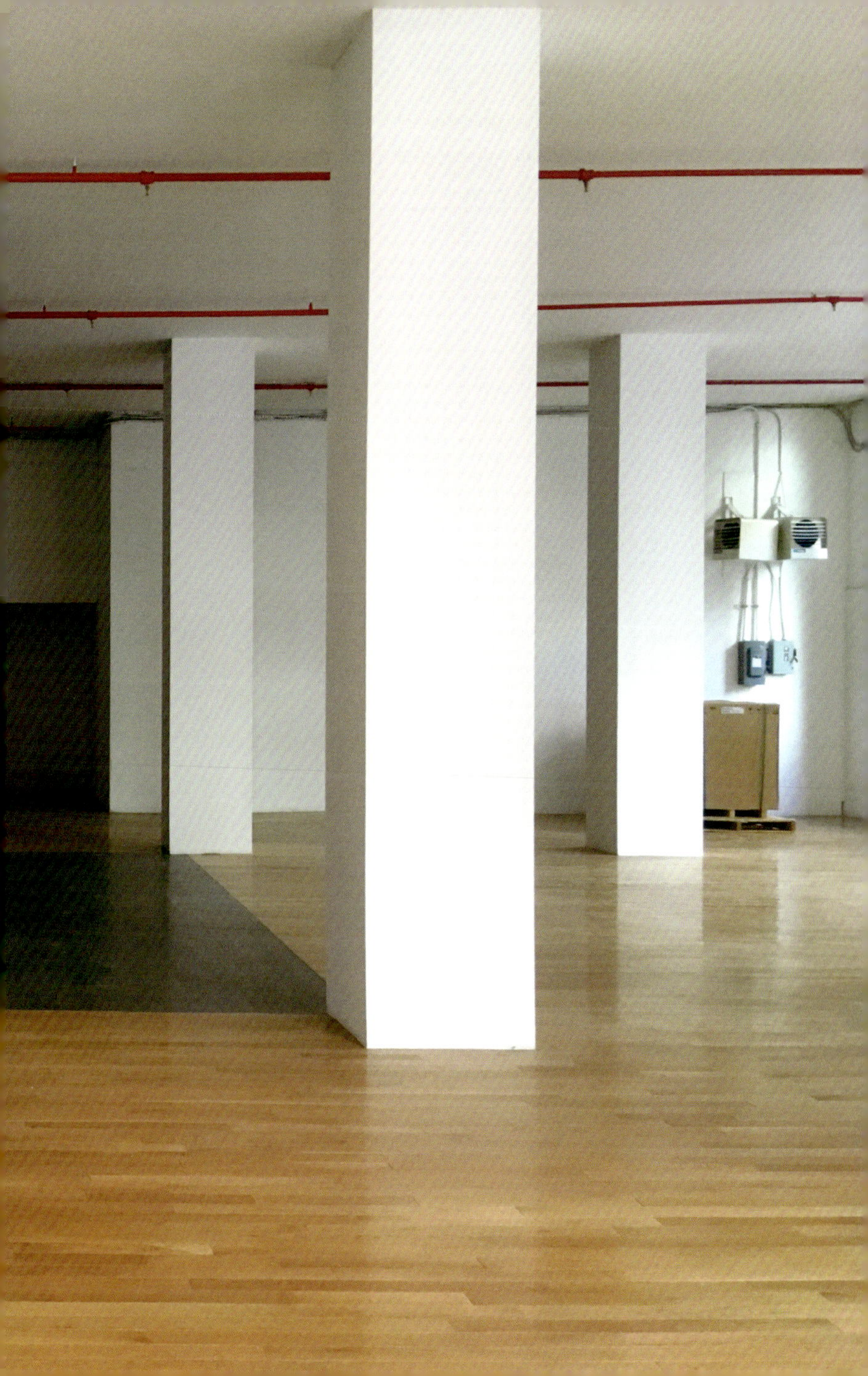

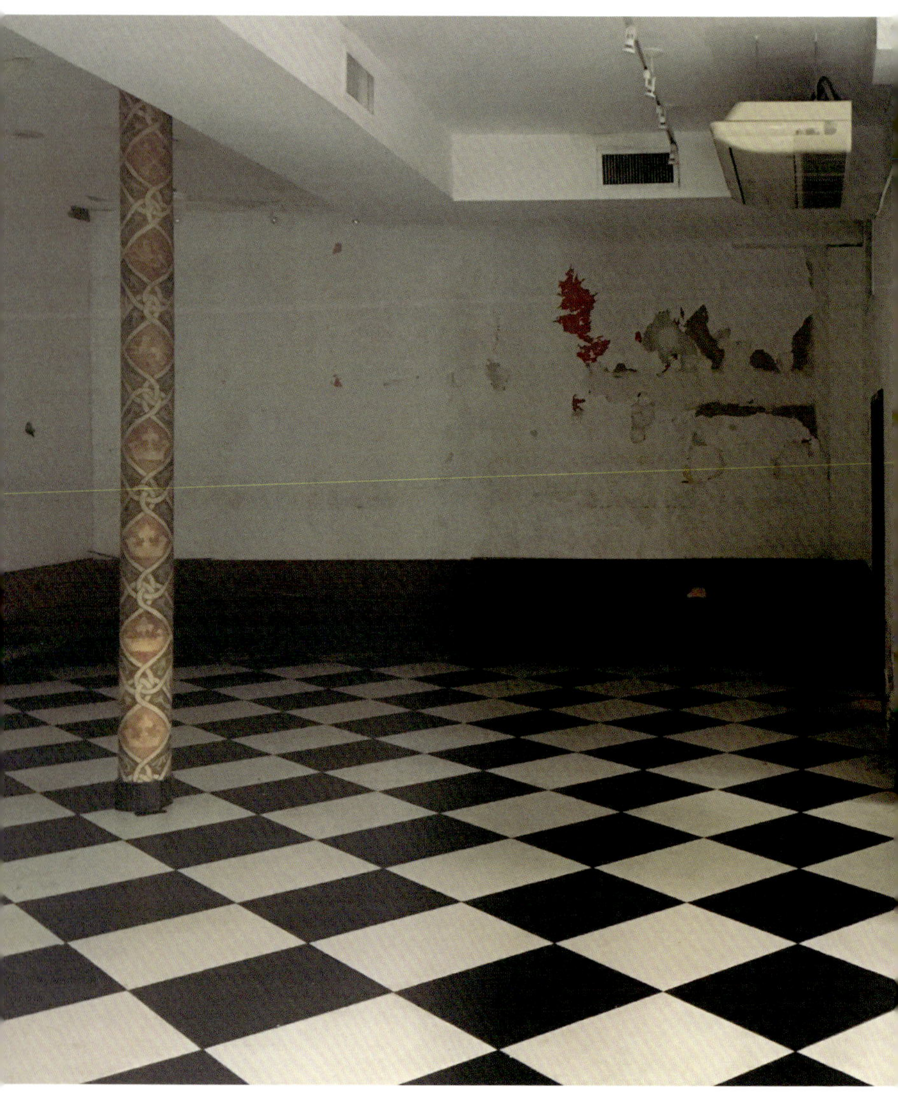

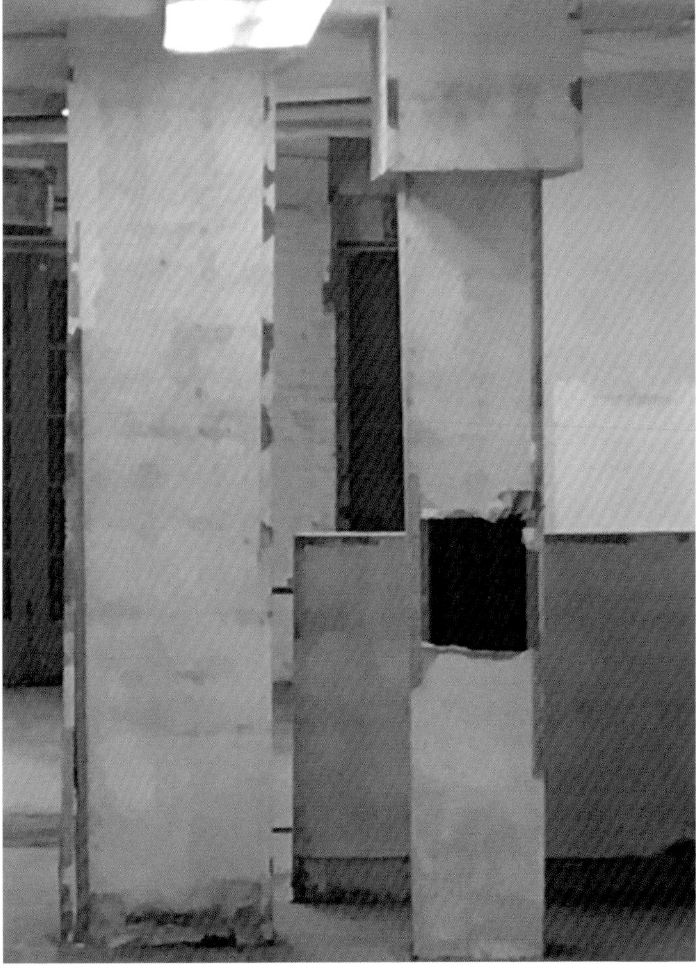

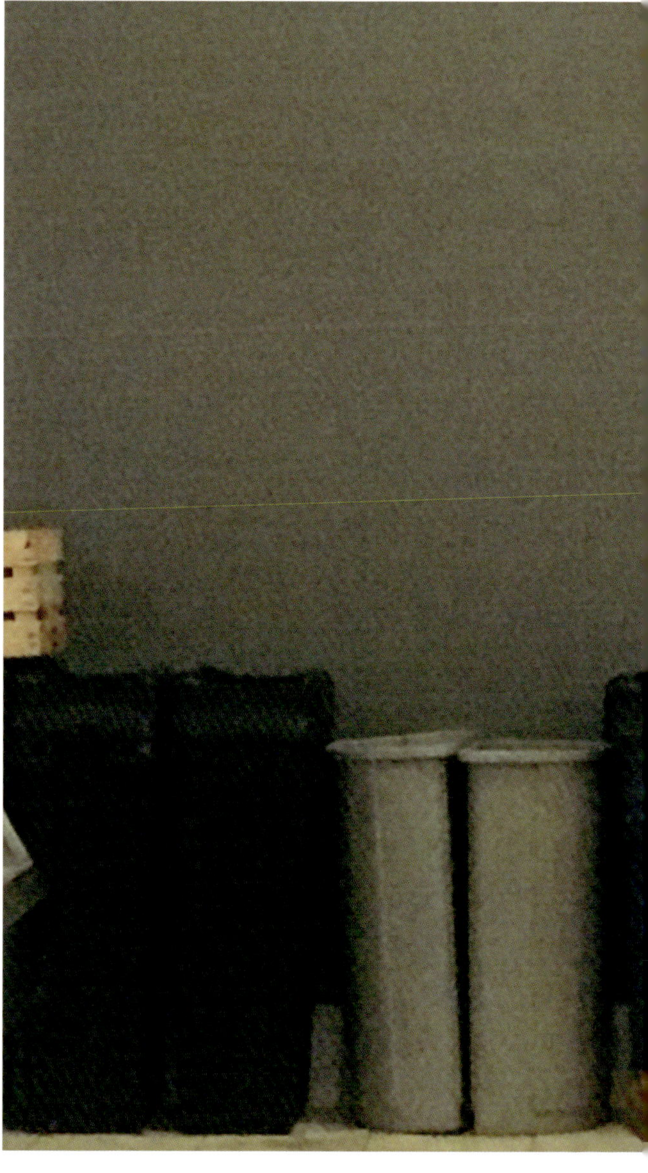

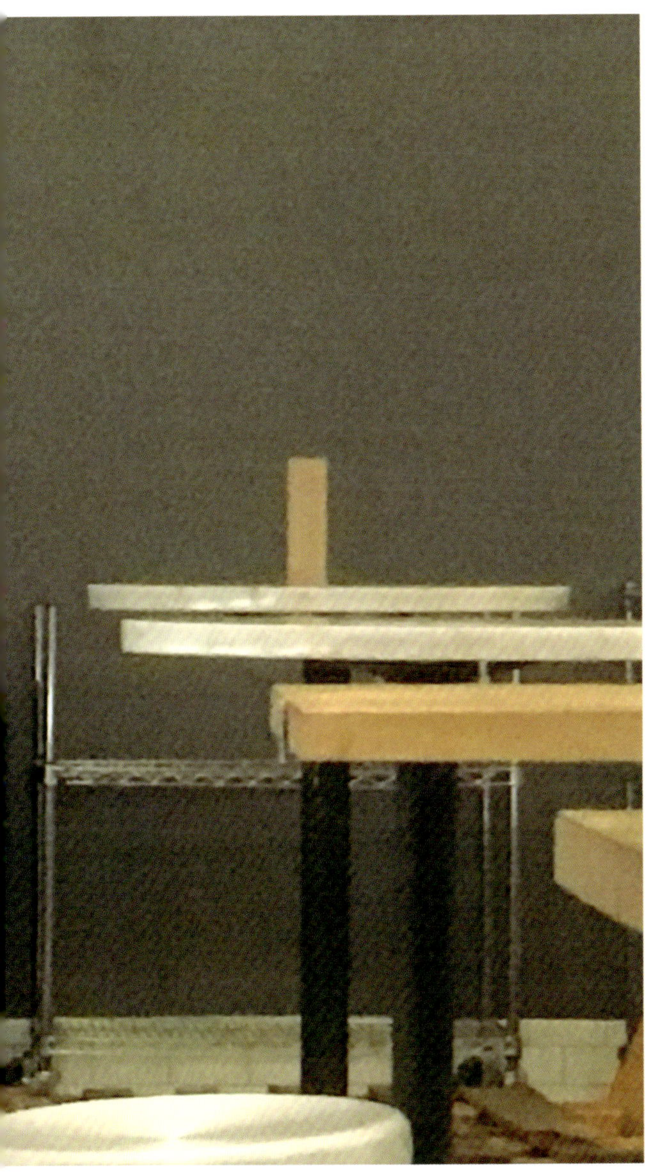

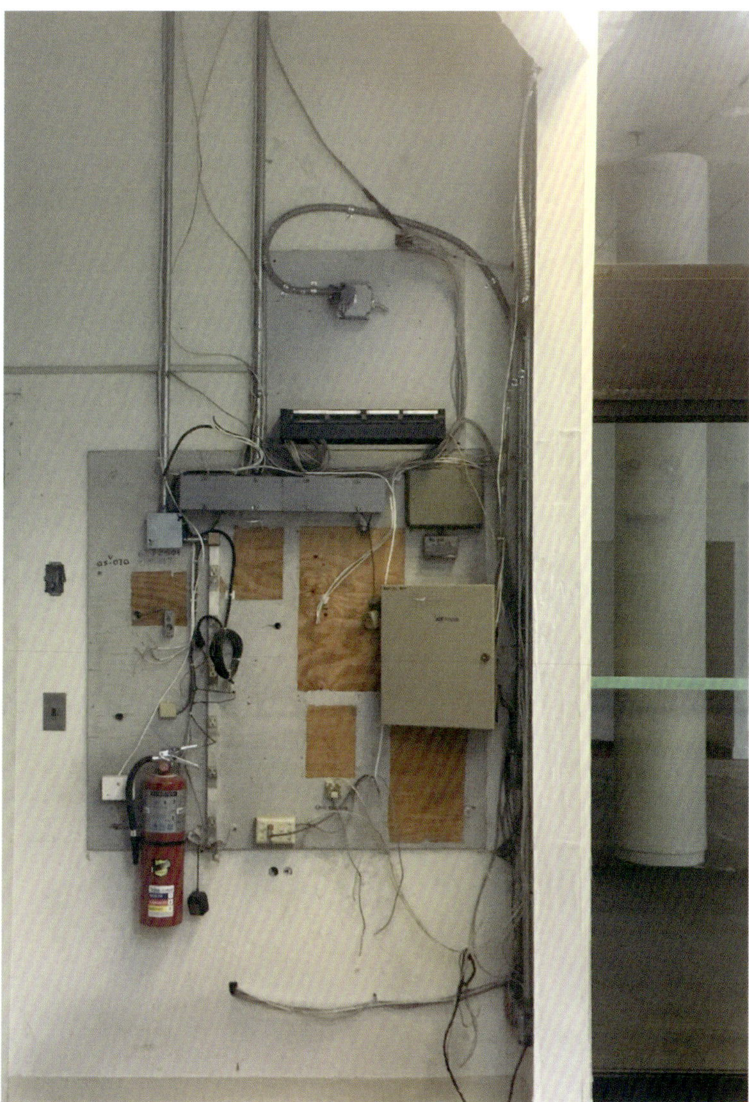

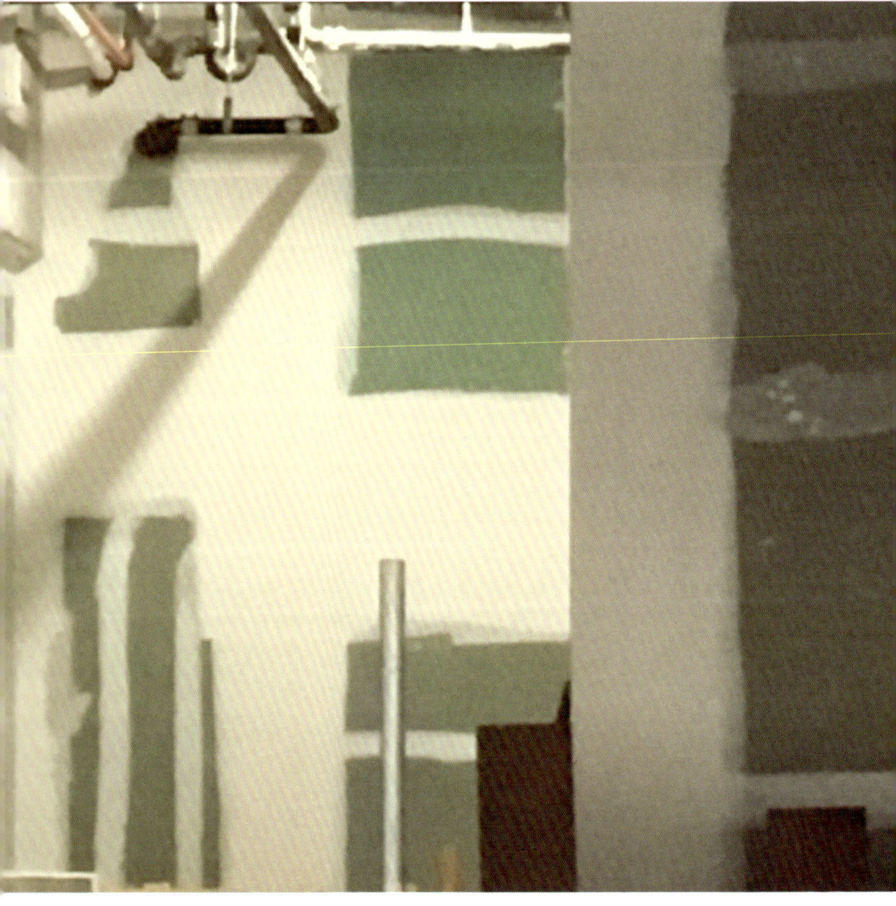

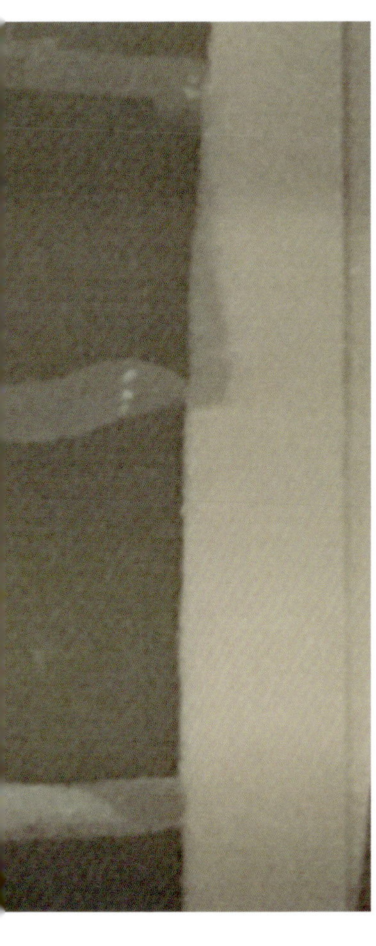

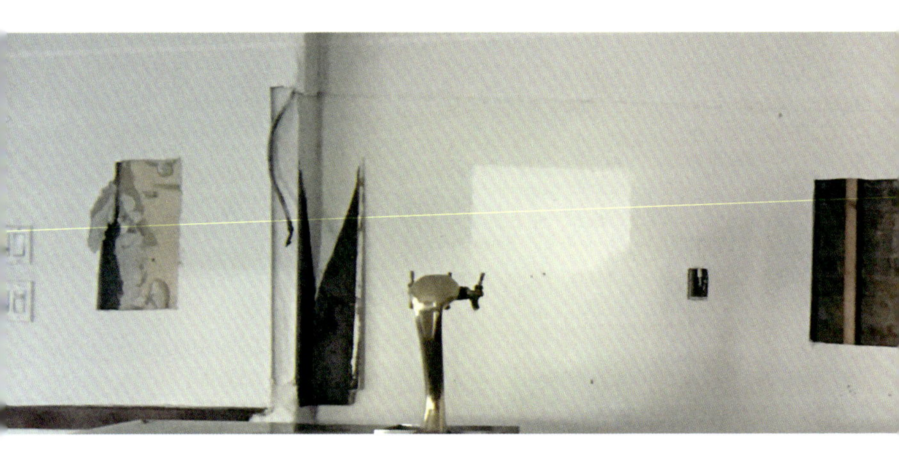

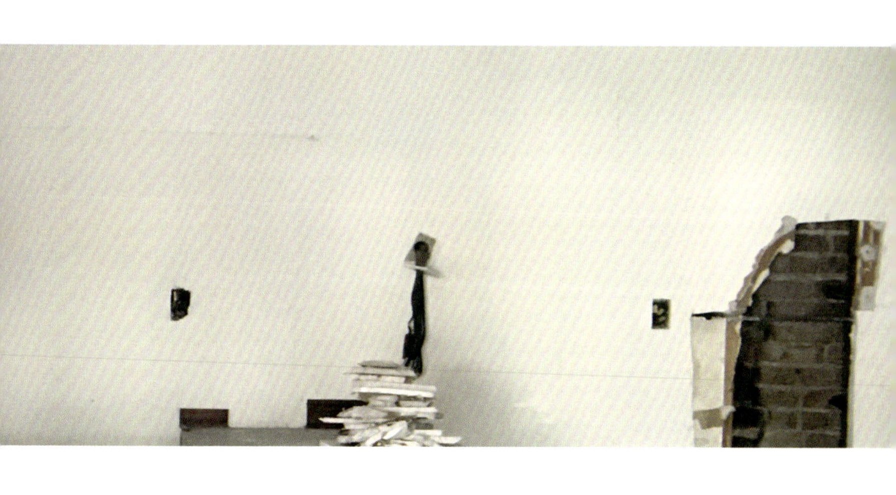

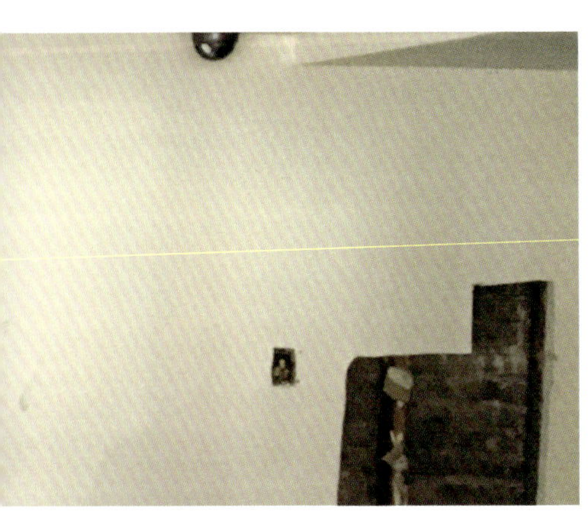

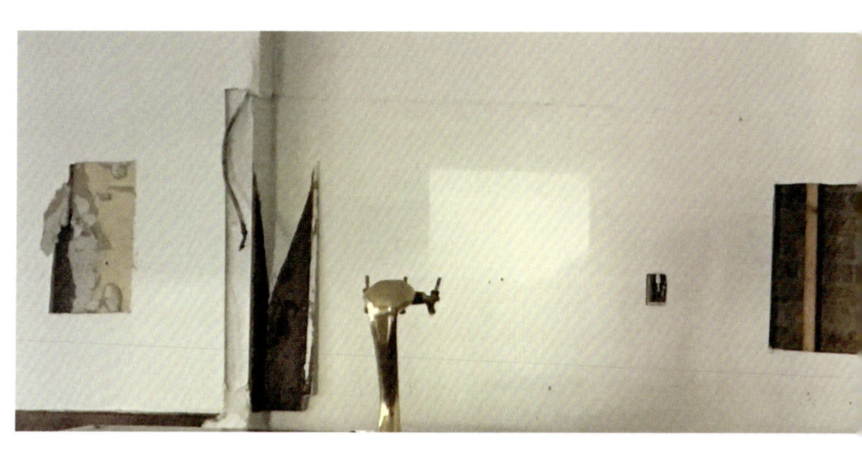

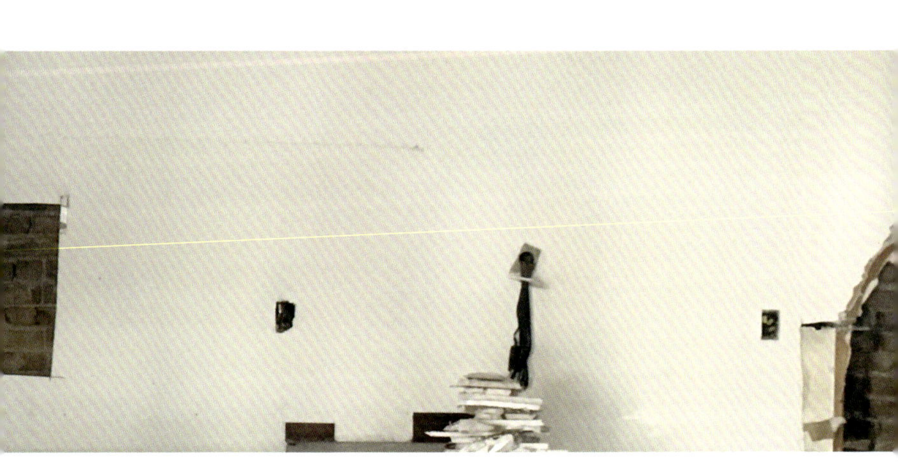

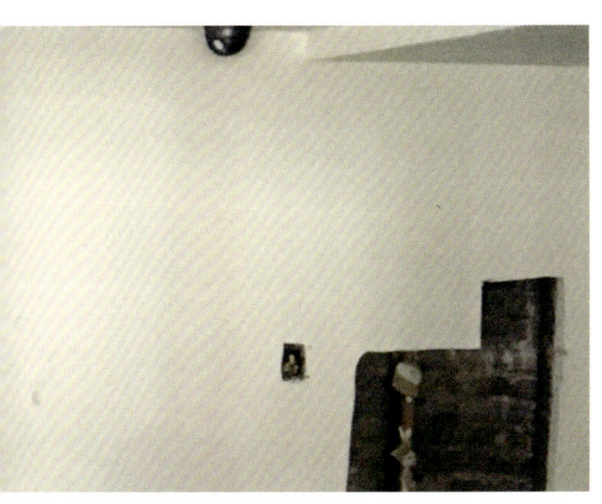

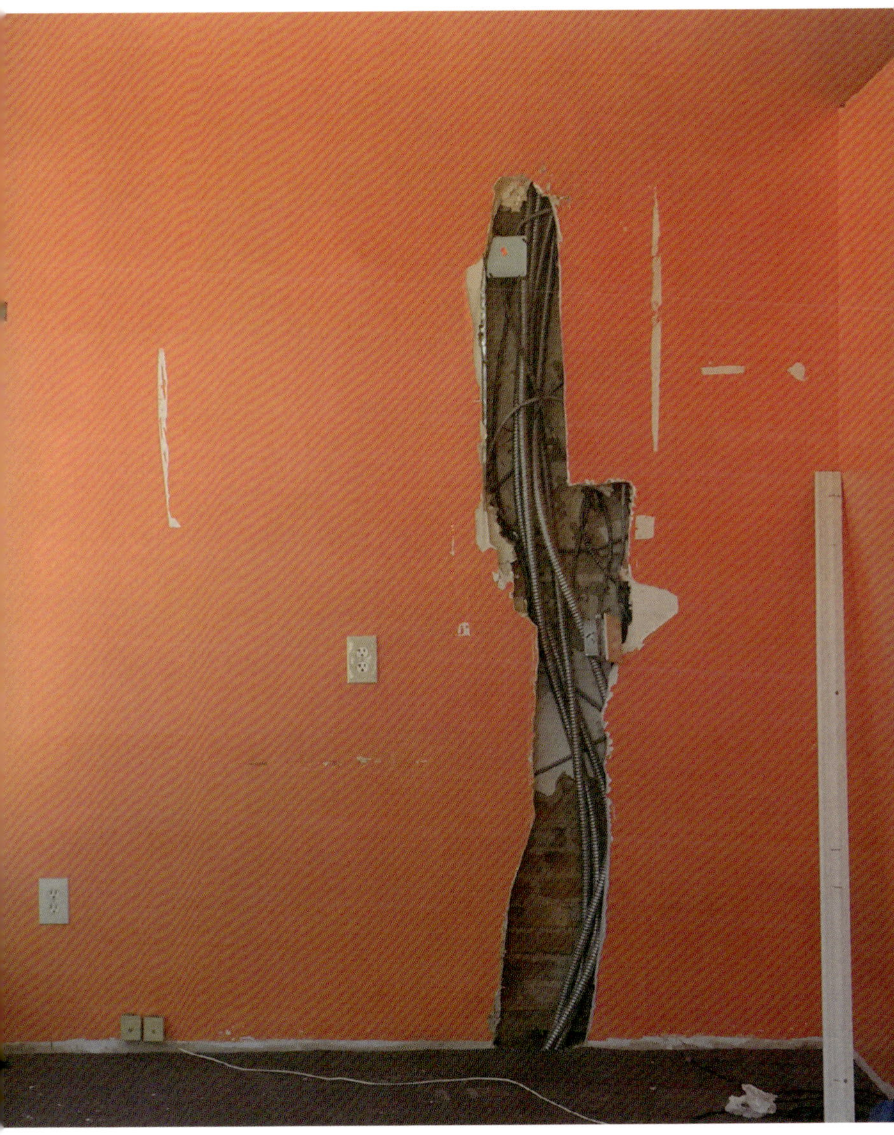

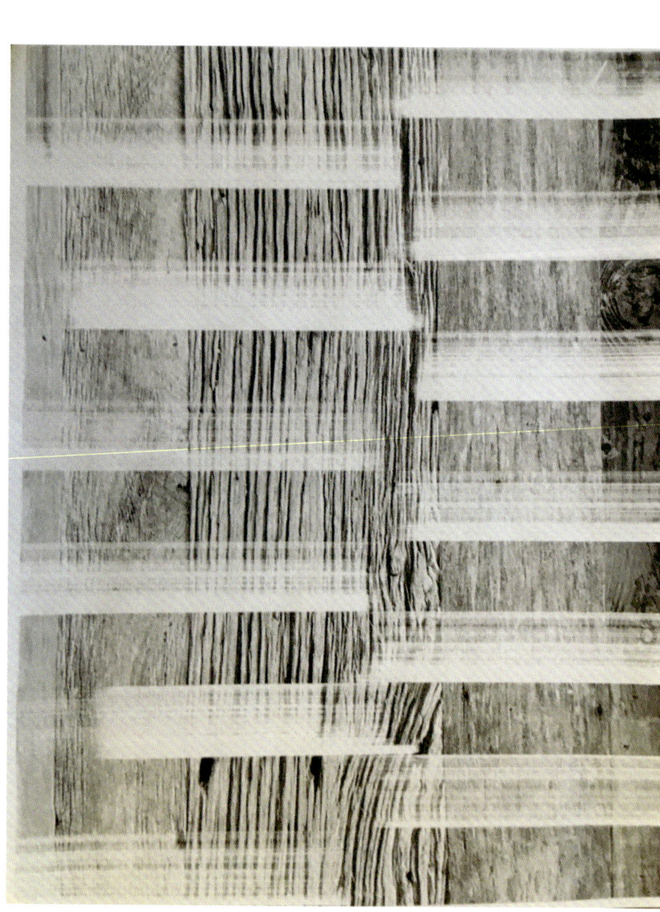

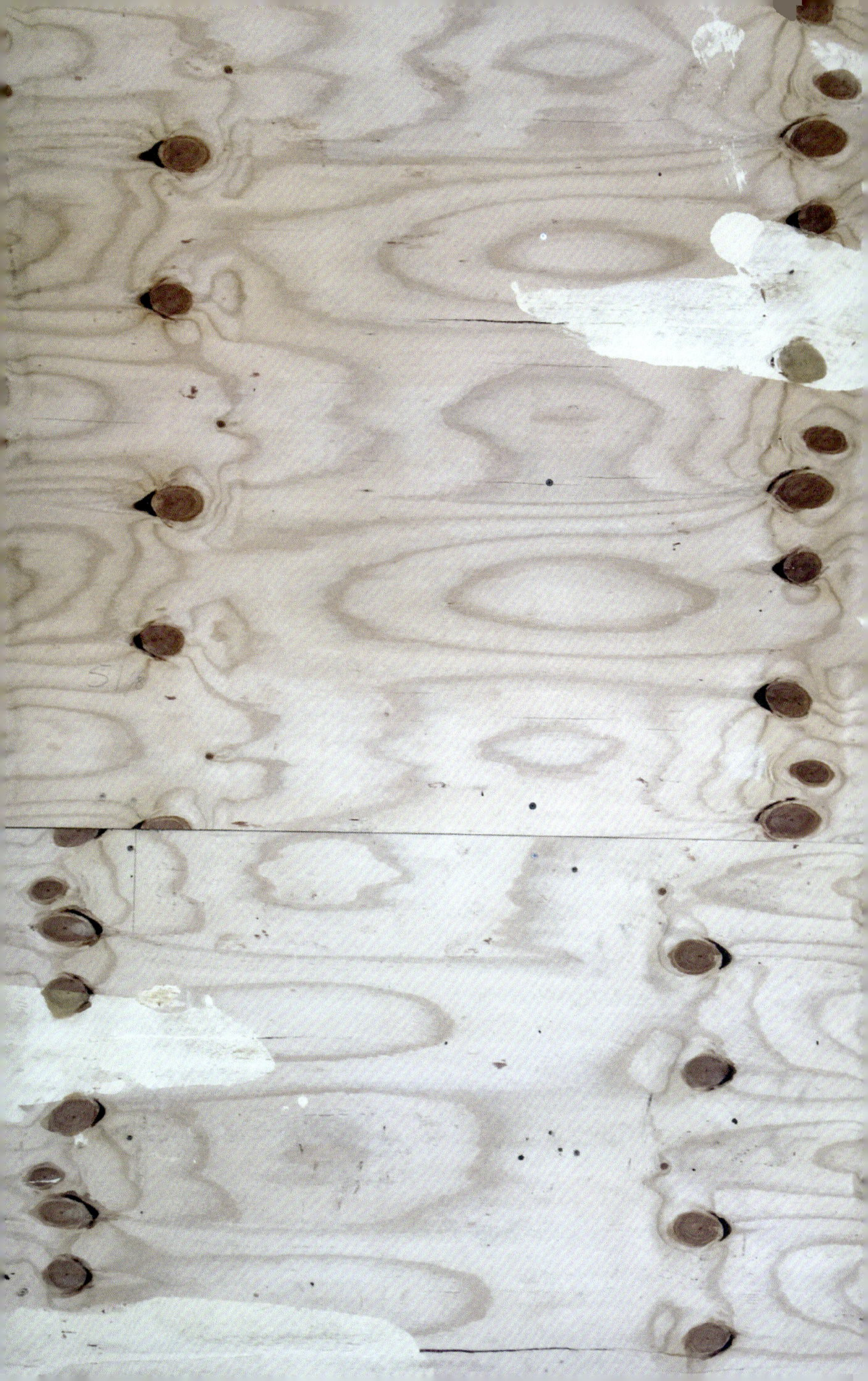

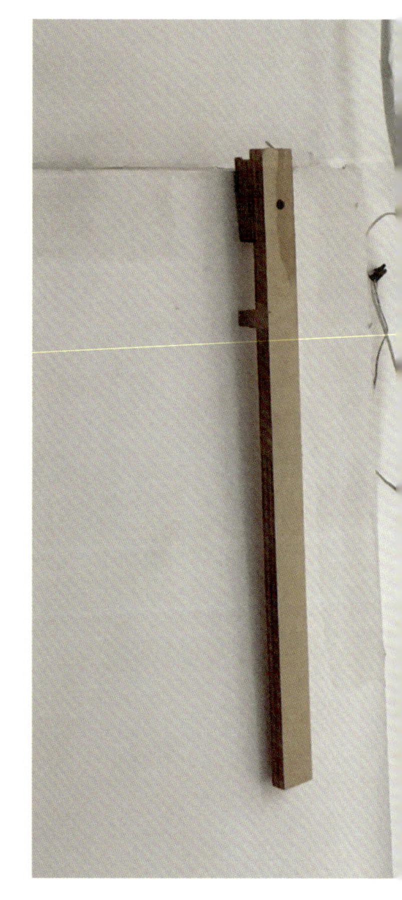

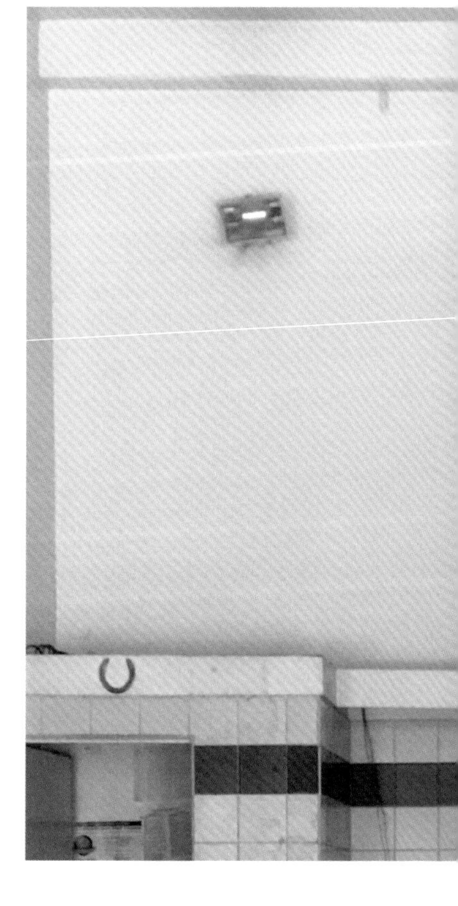

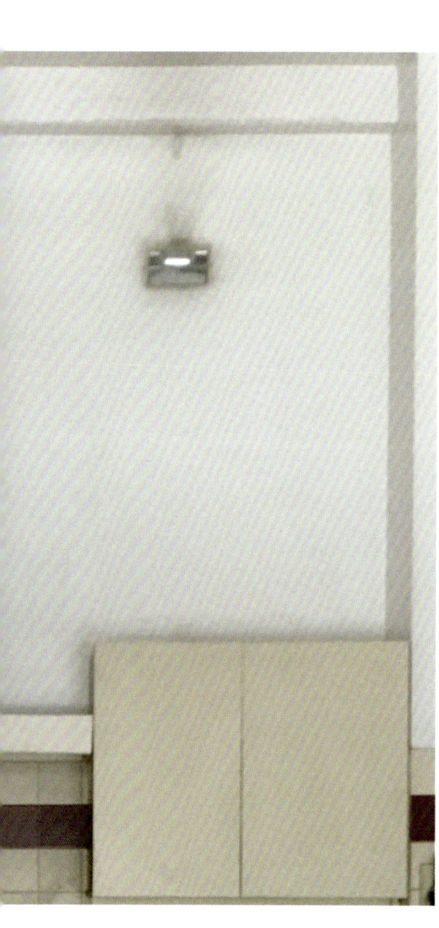

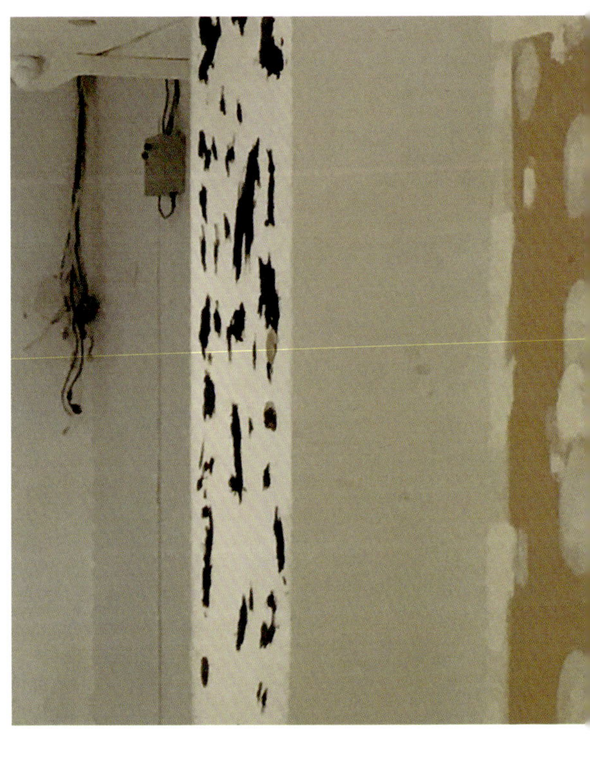

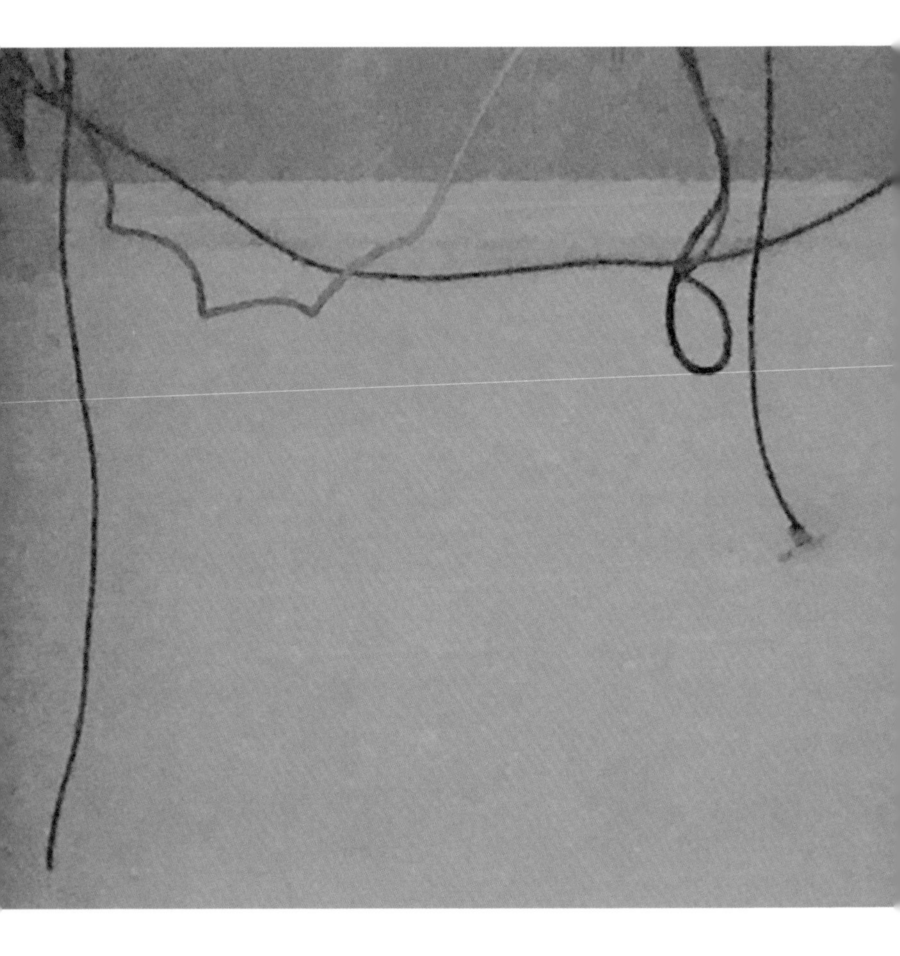

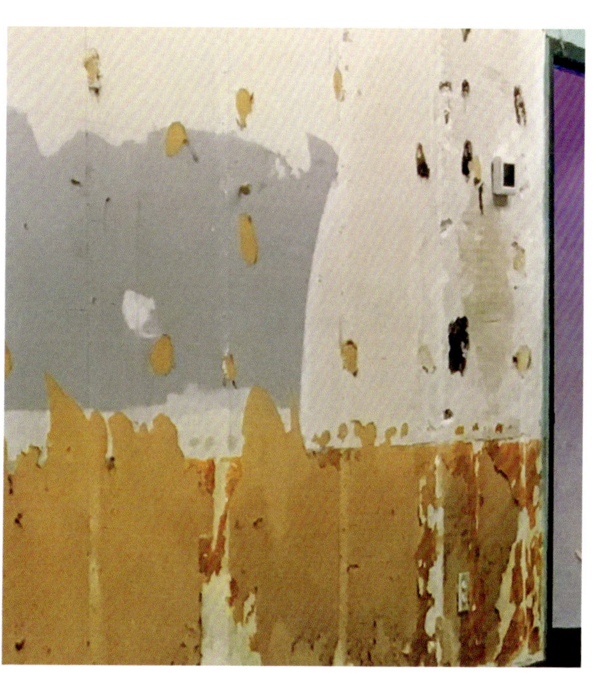

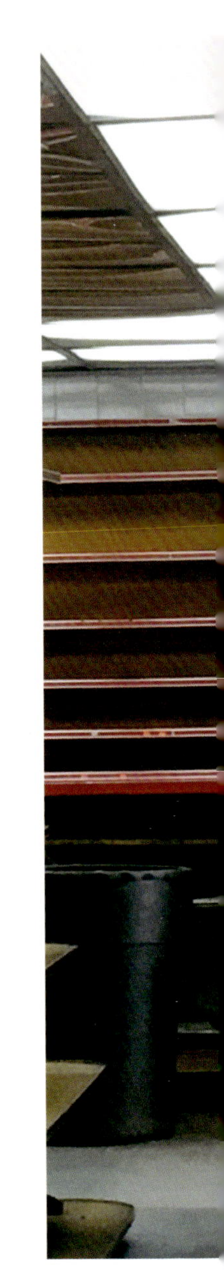

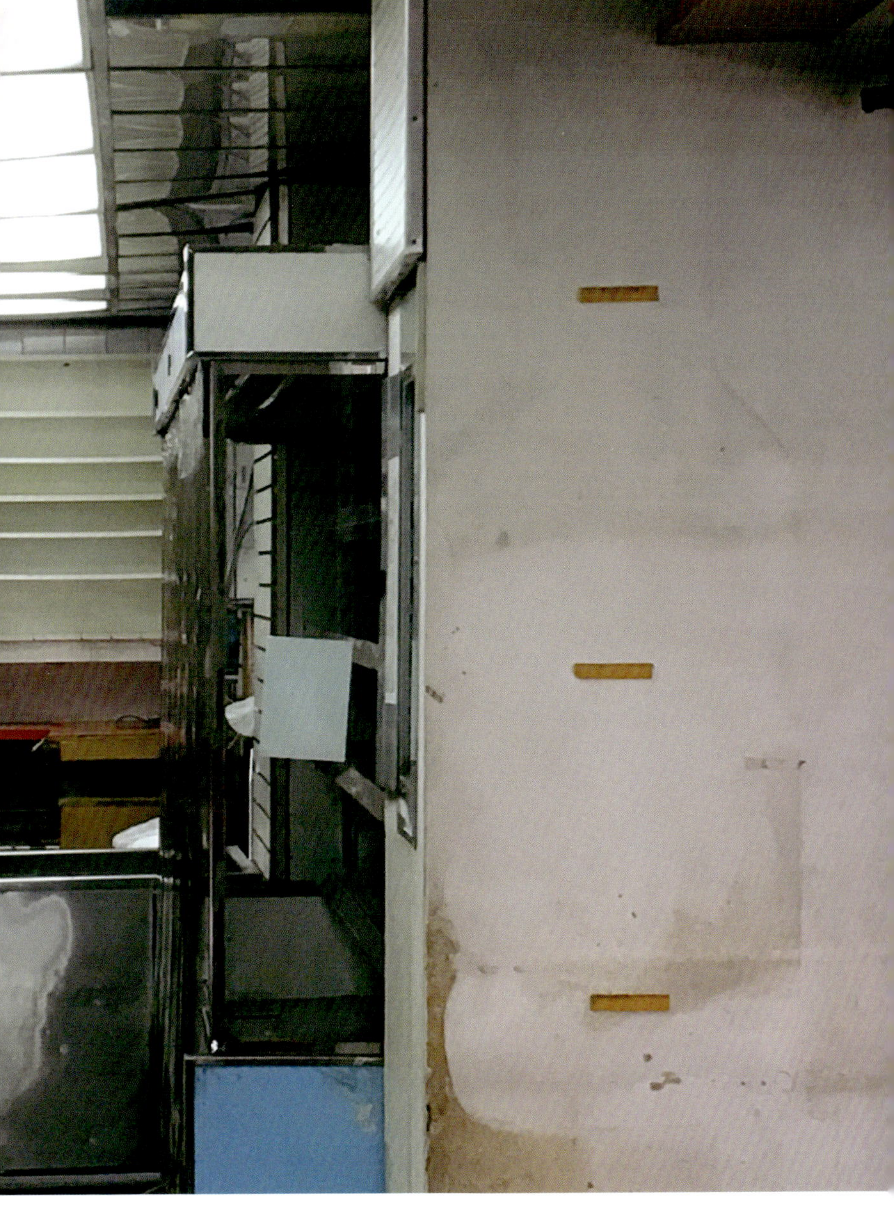

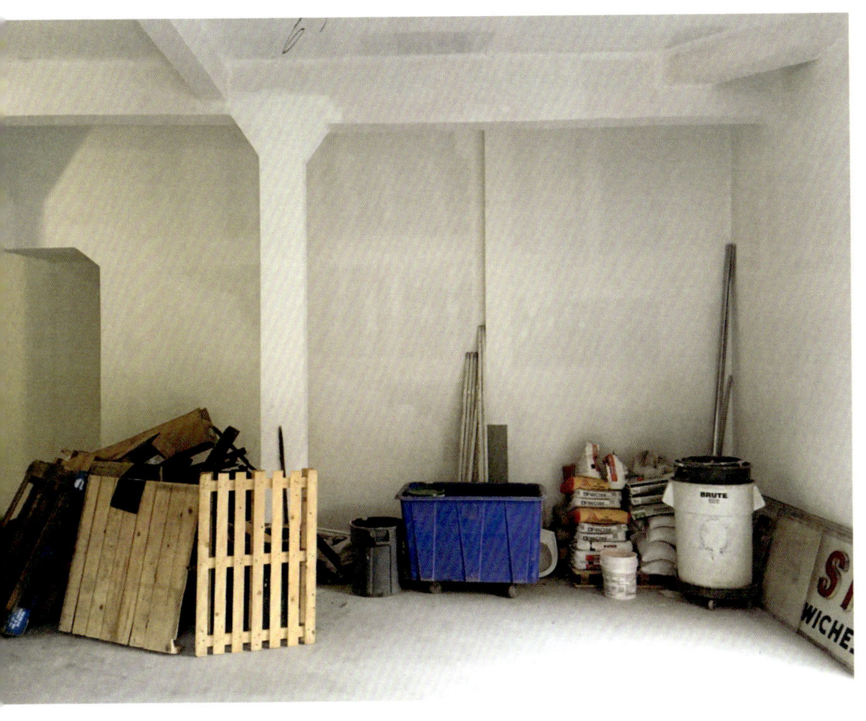
BRUTE

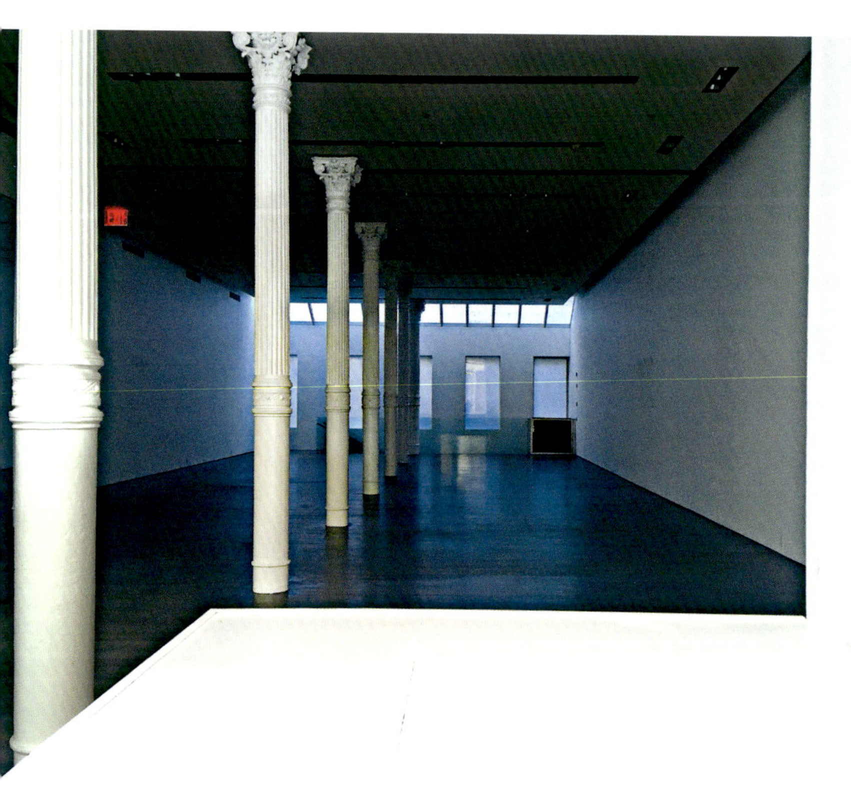

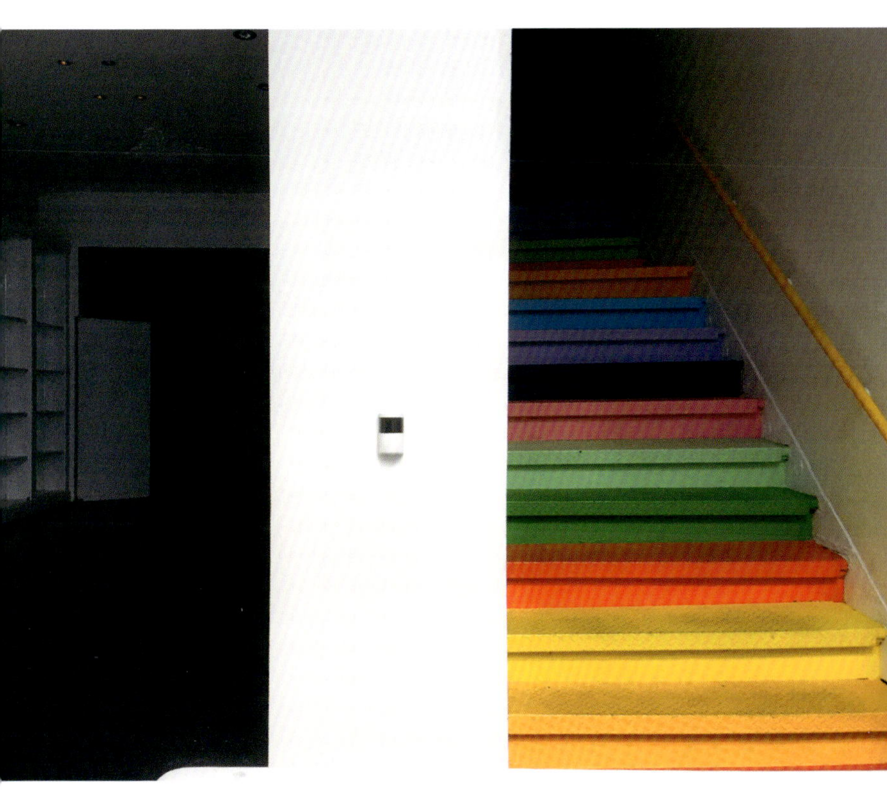

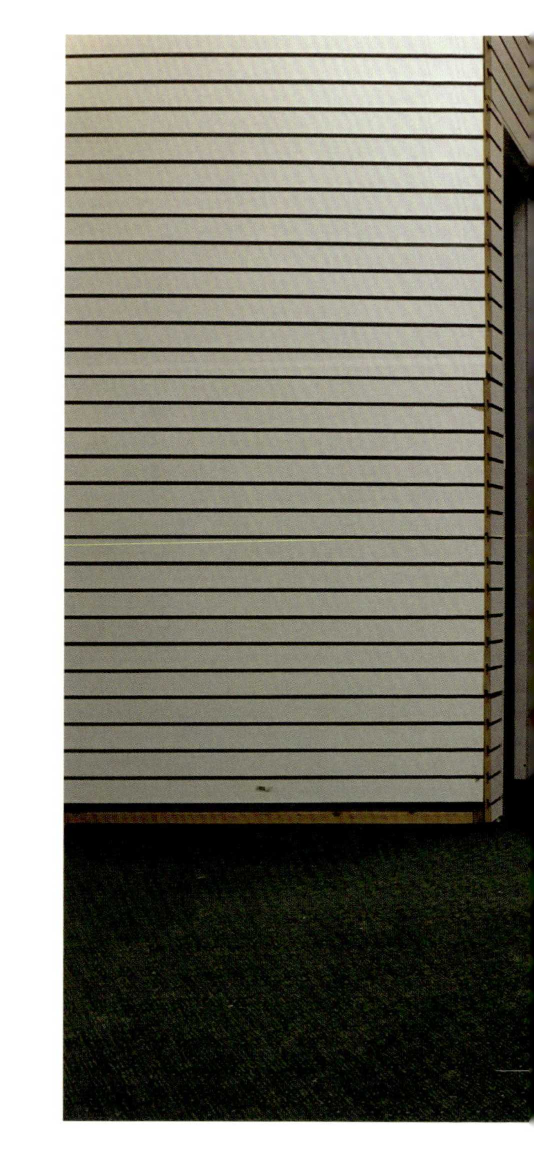

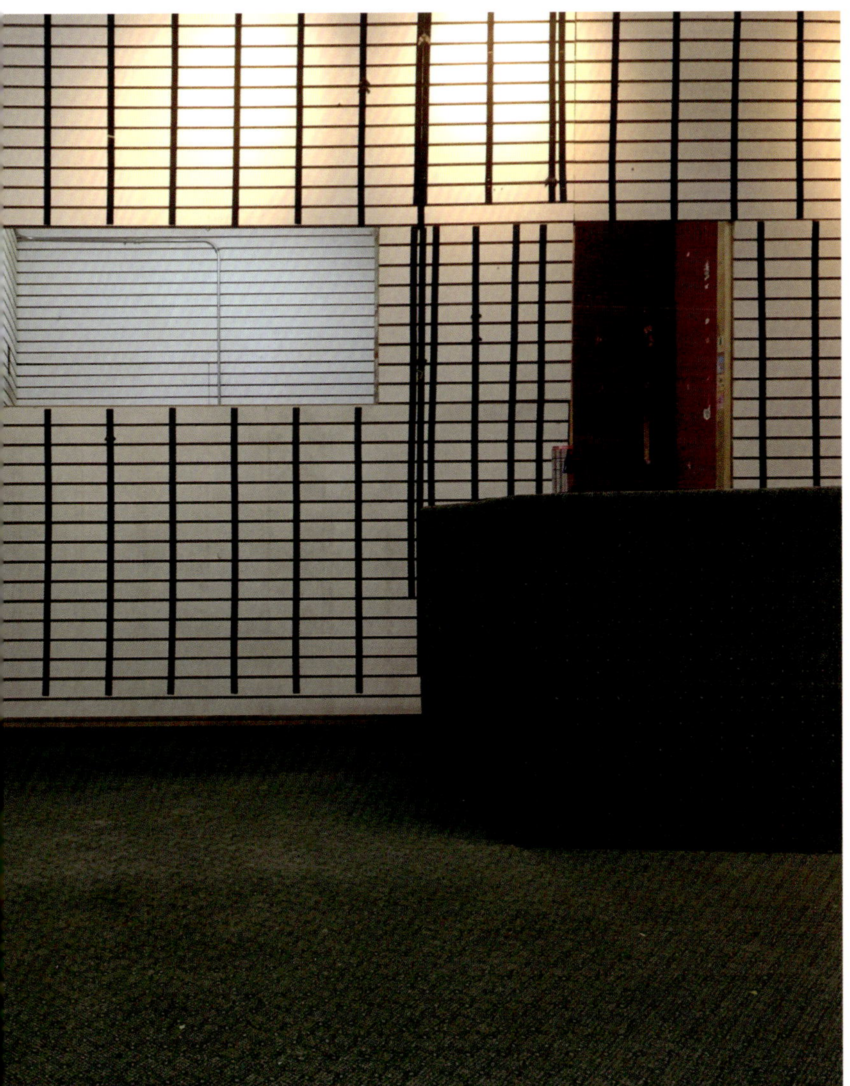

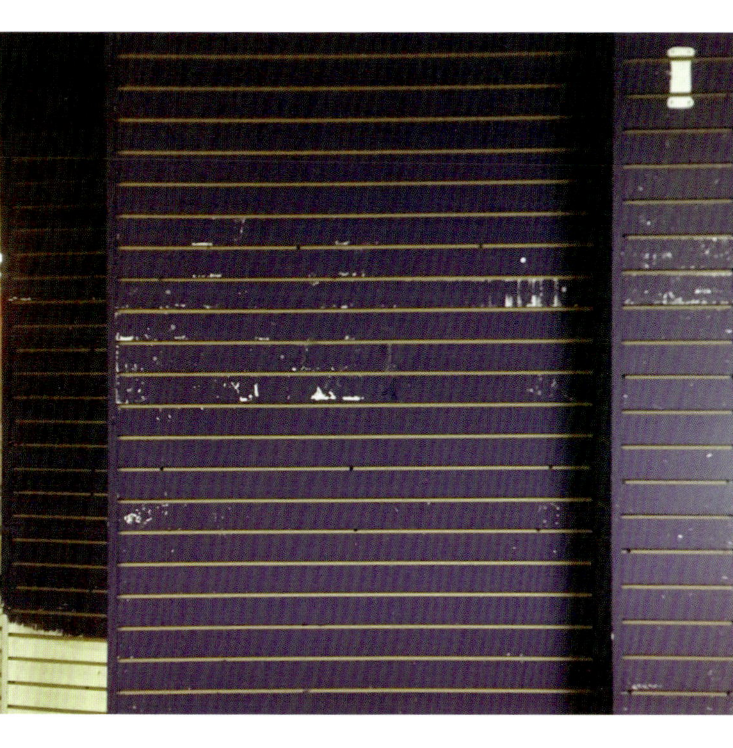

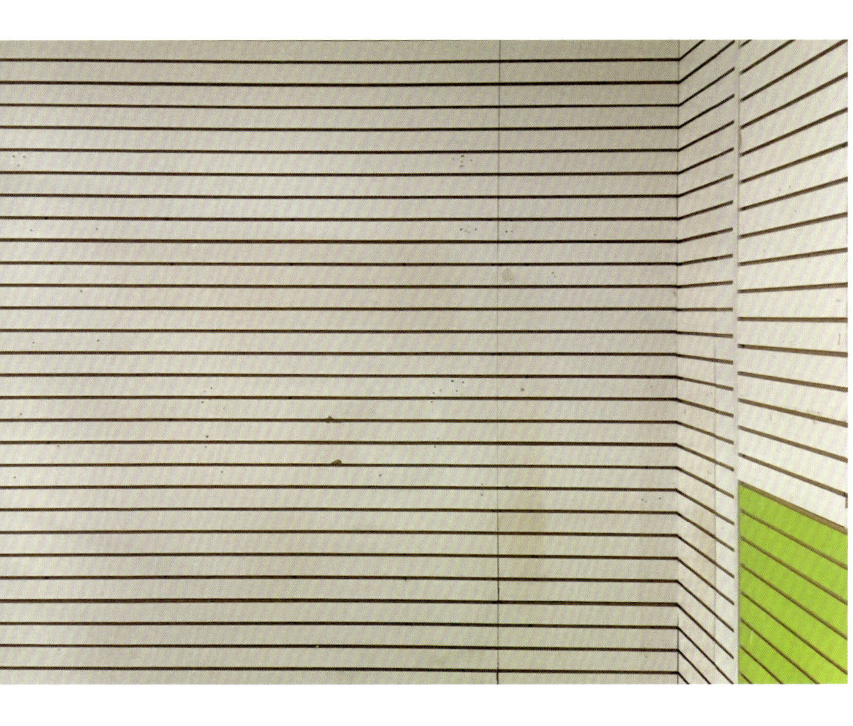

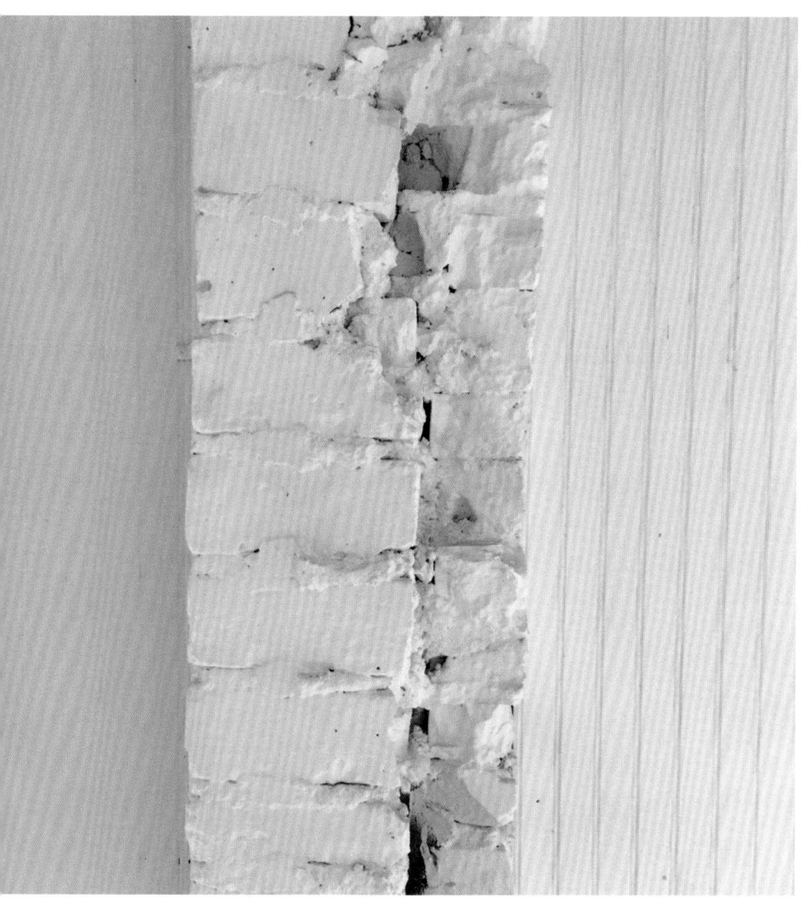

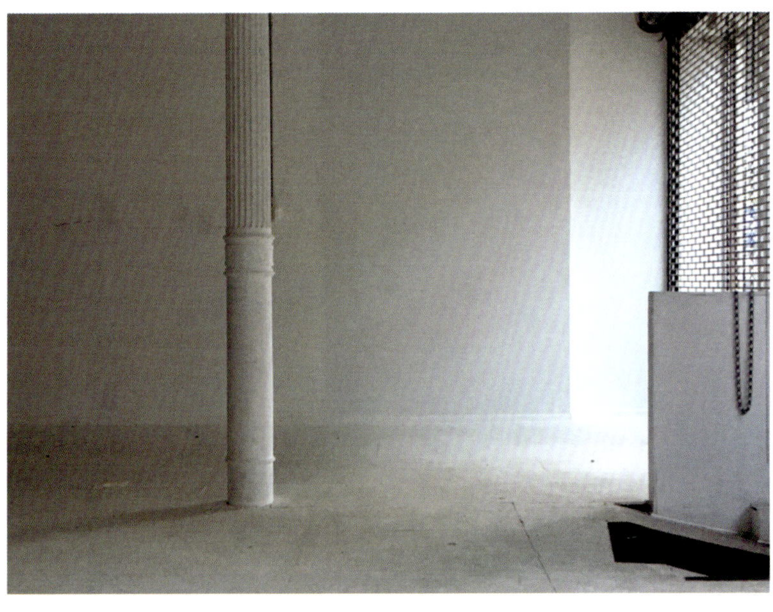

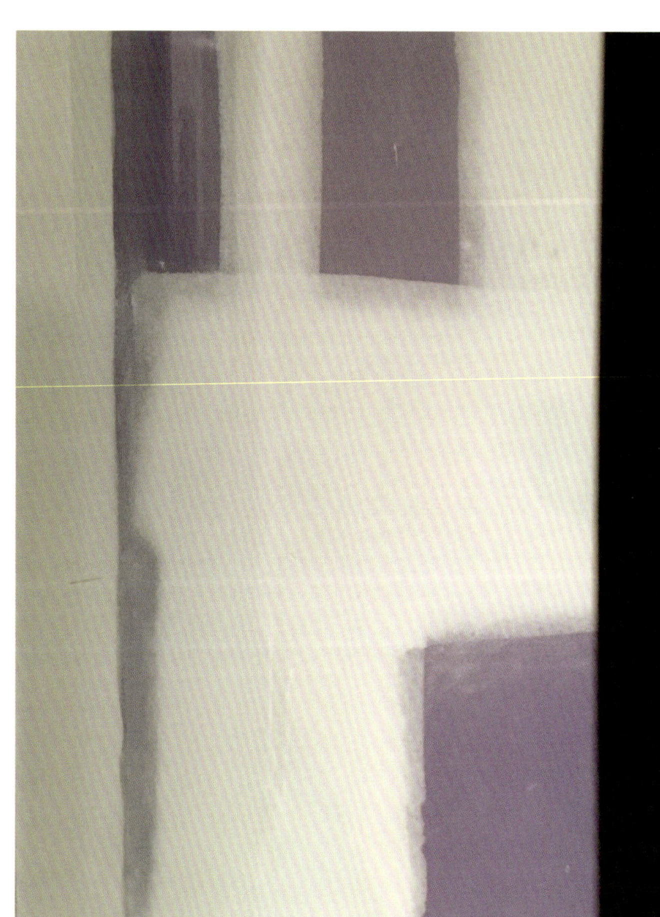

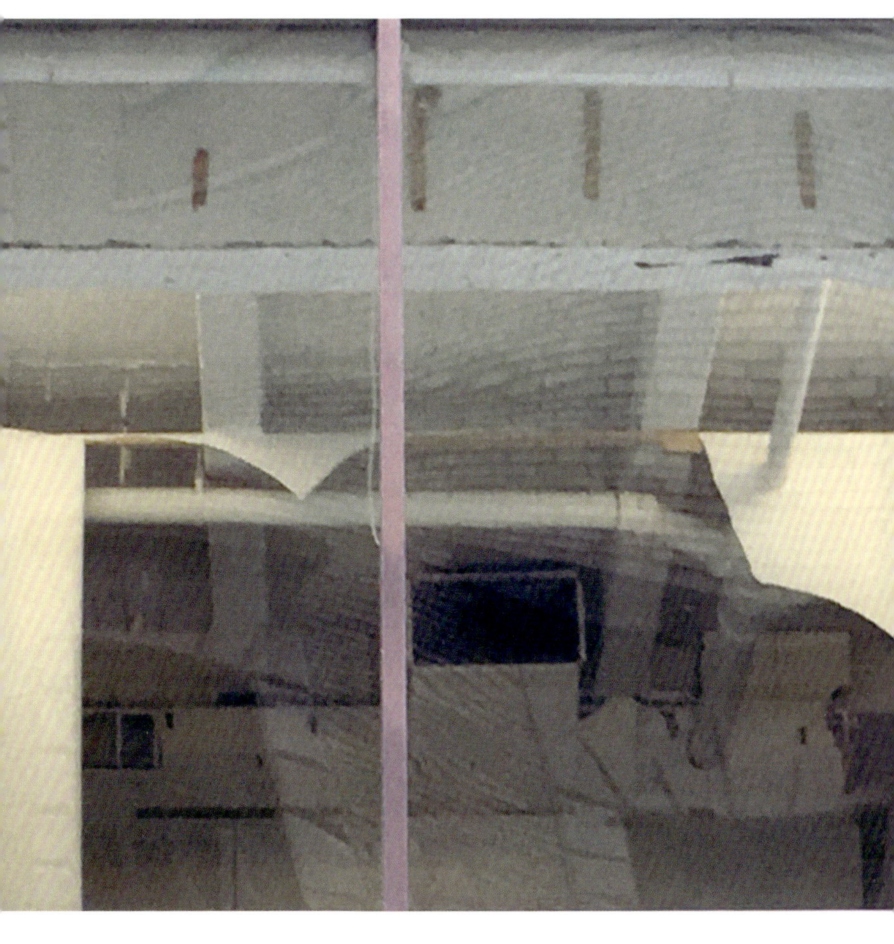

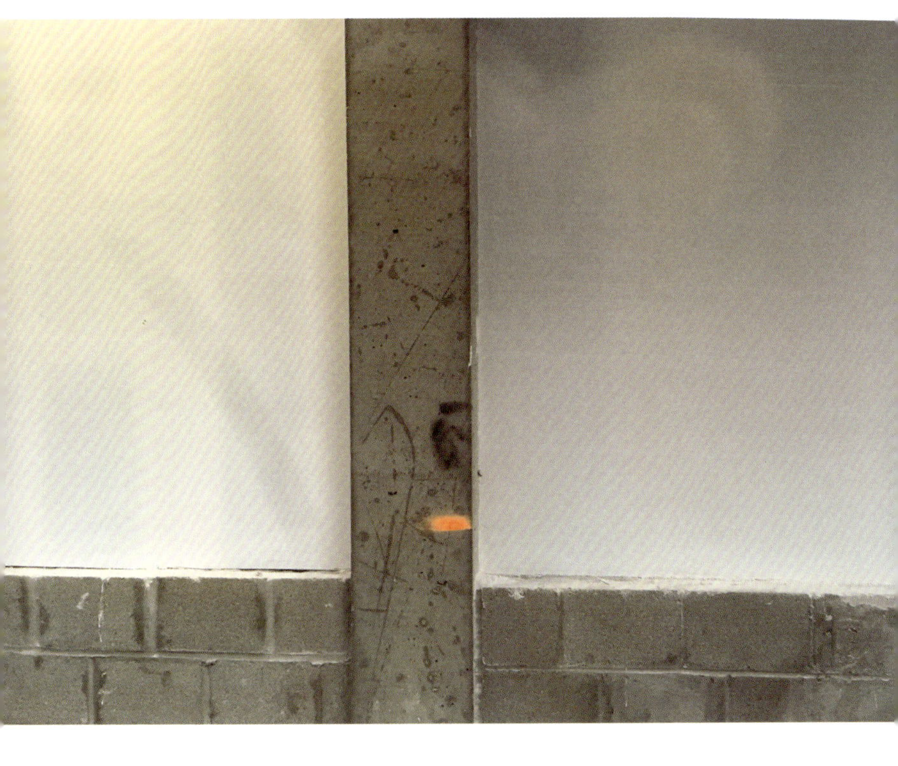

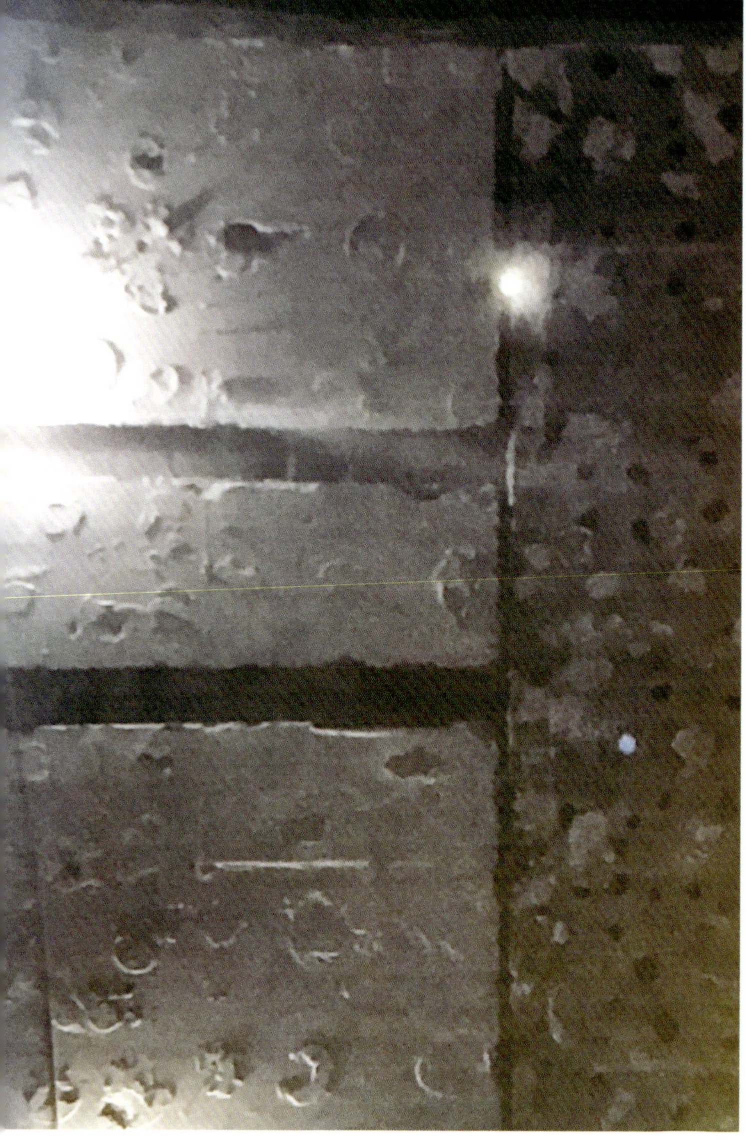

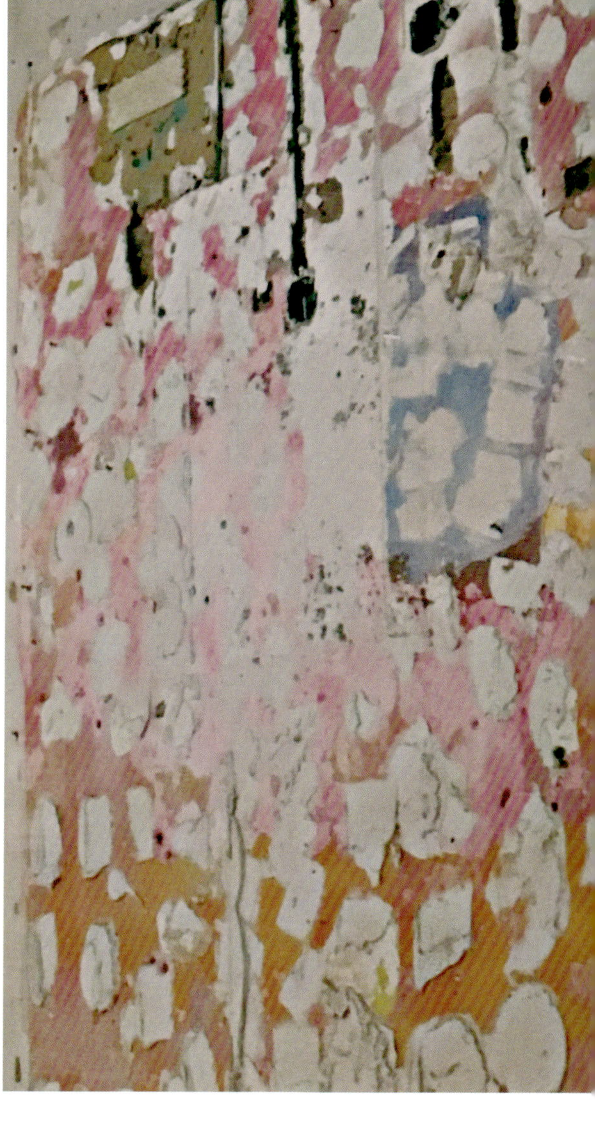

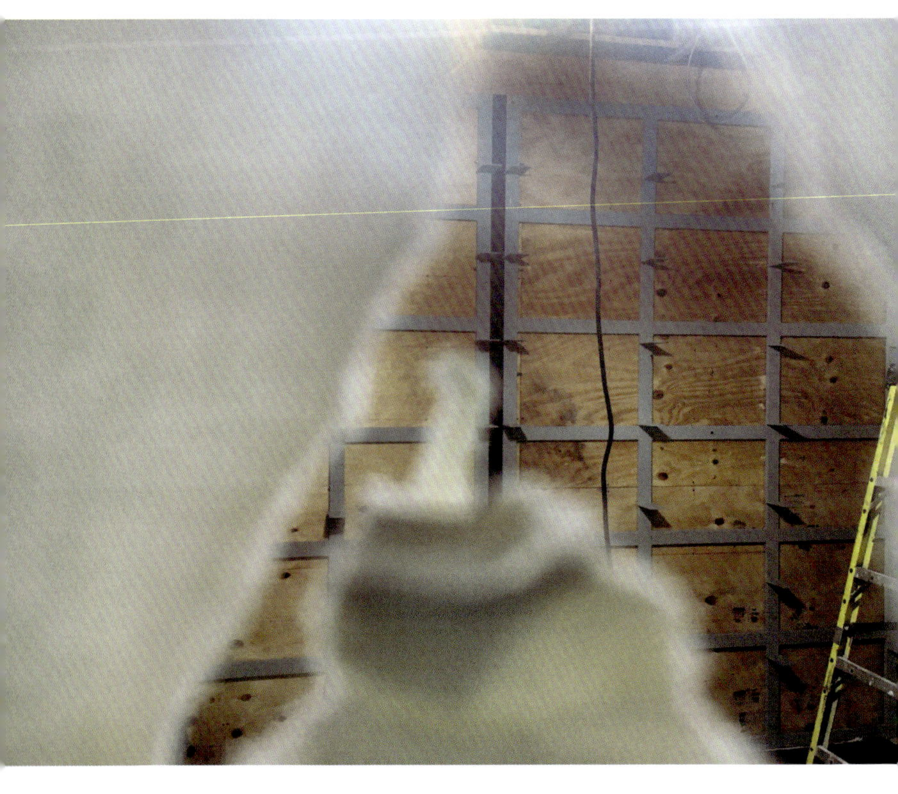

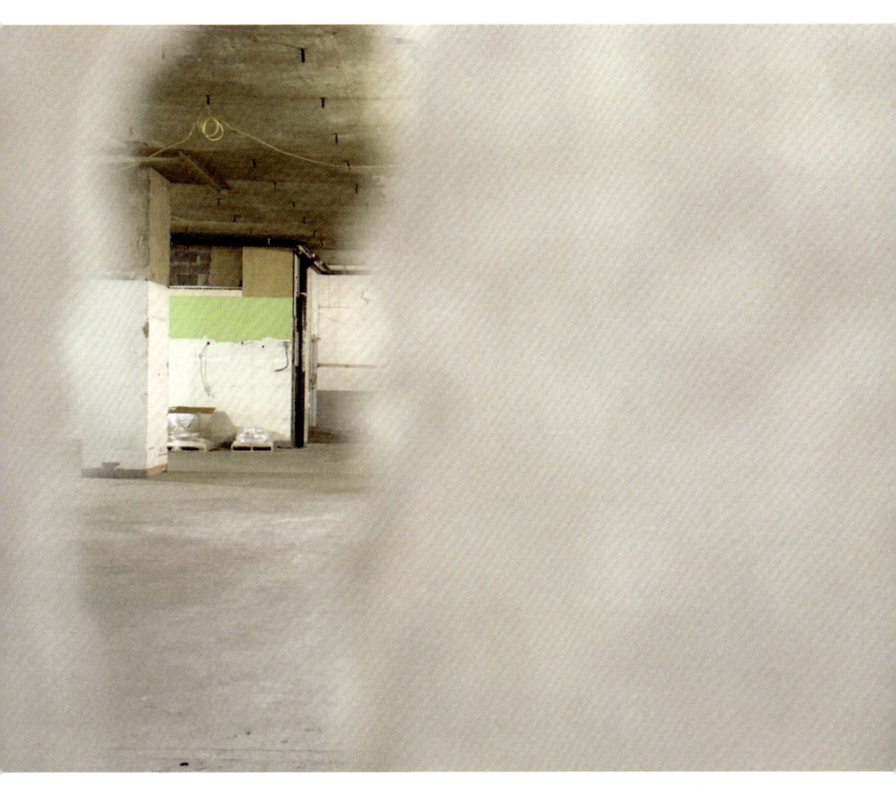

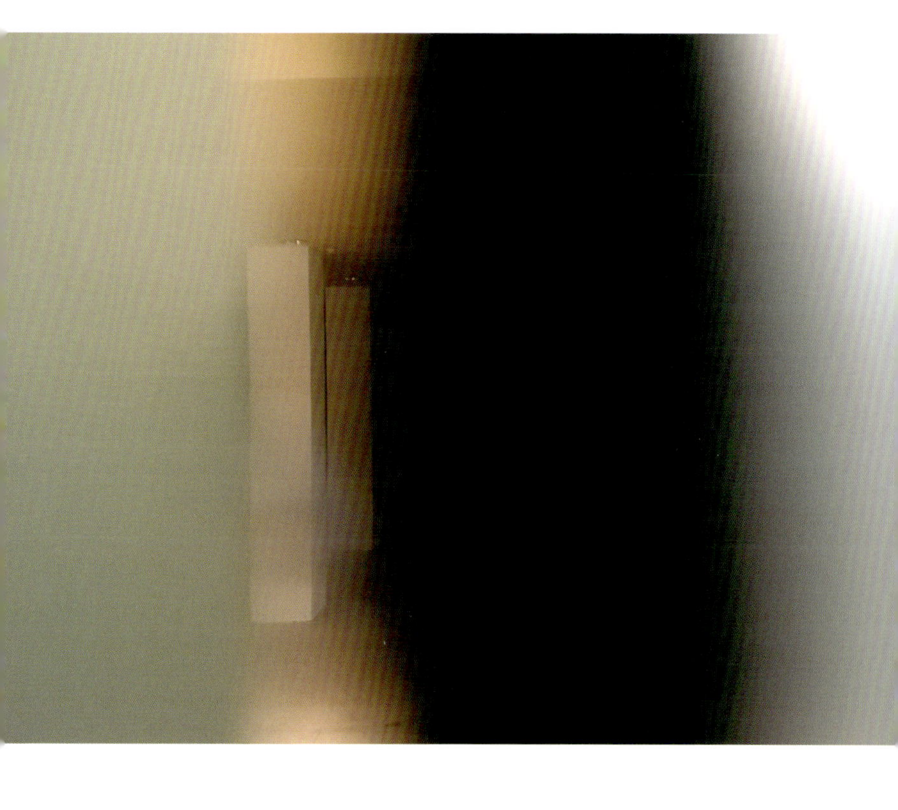

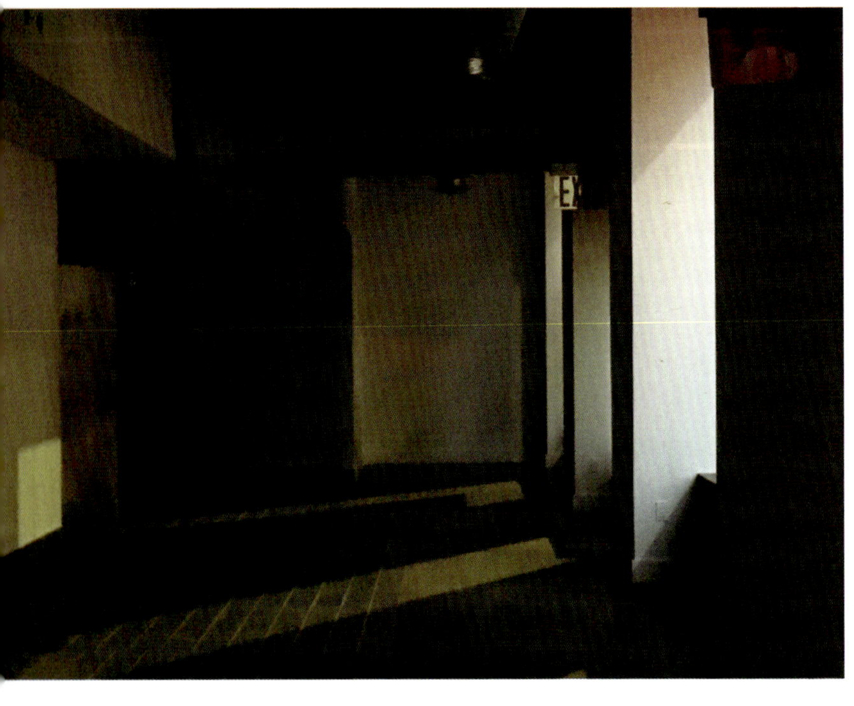

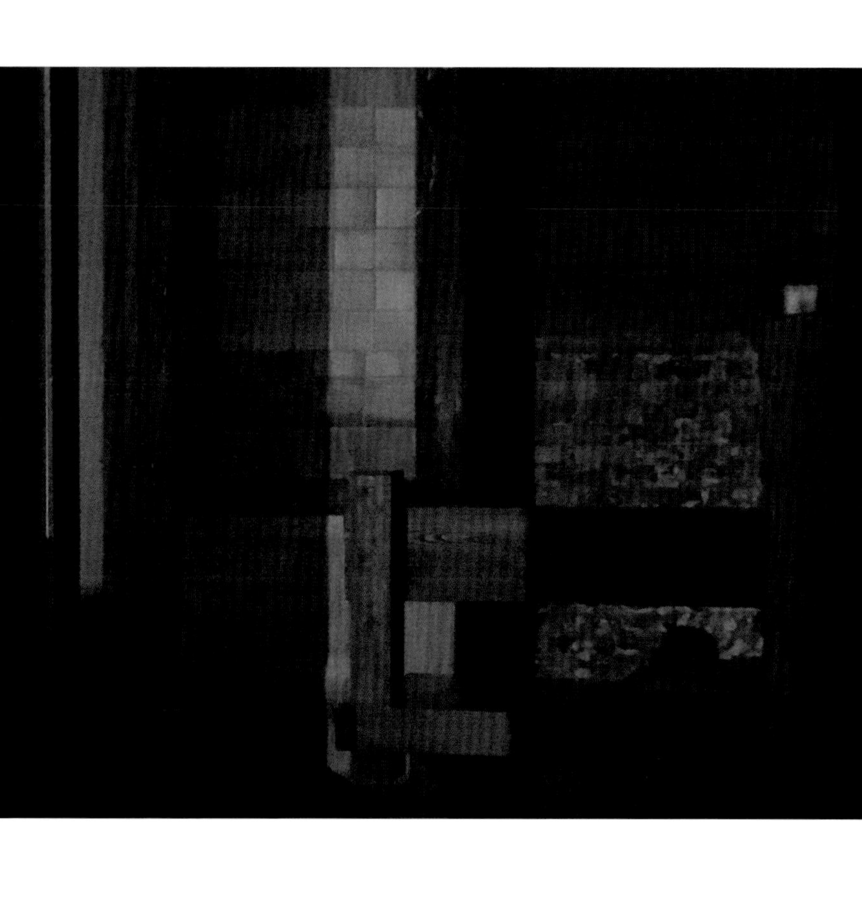

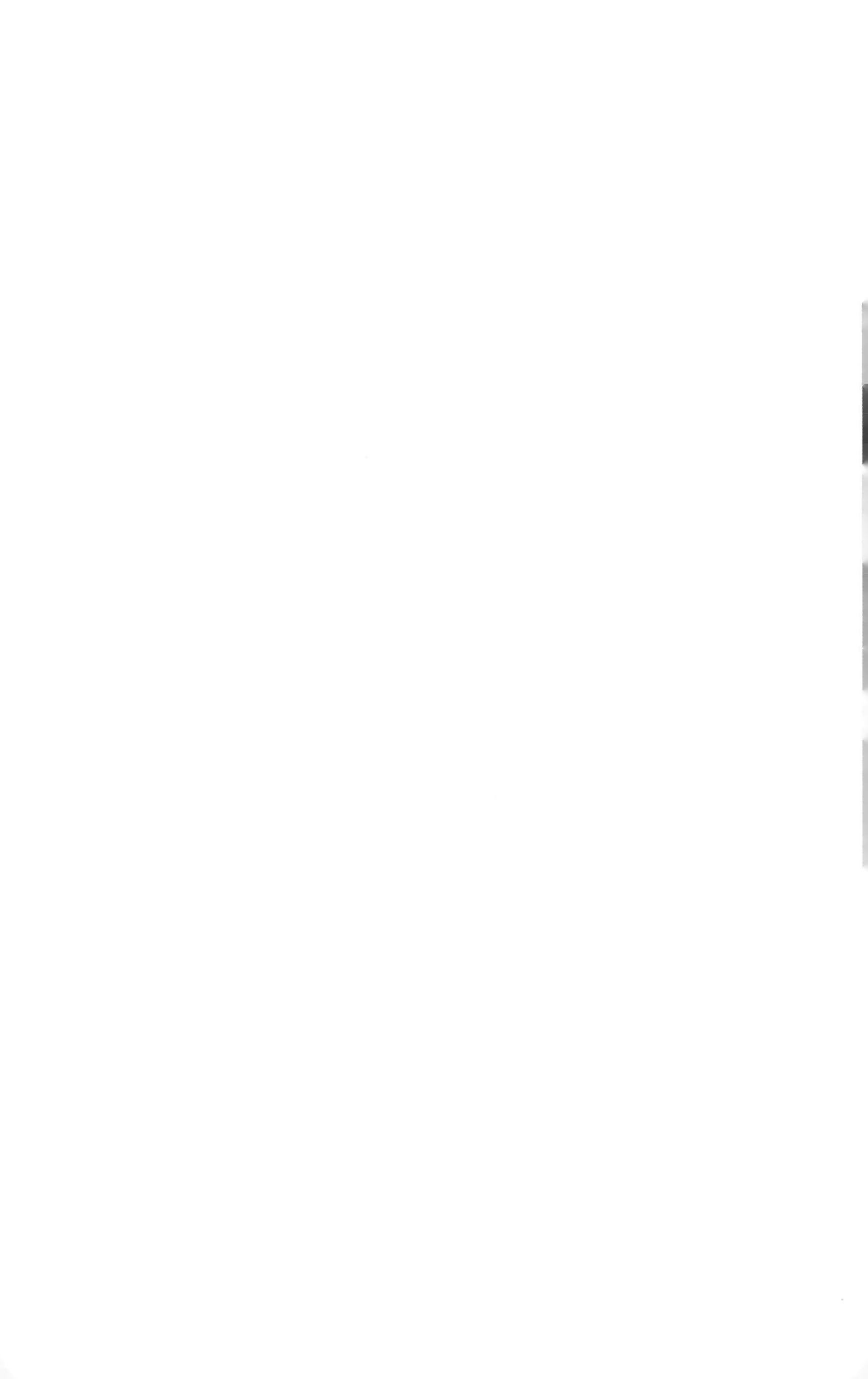

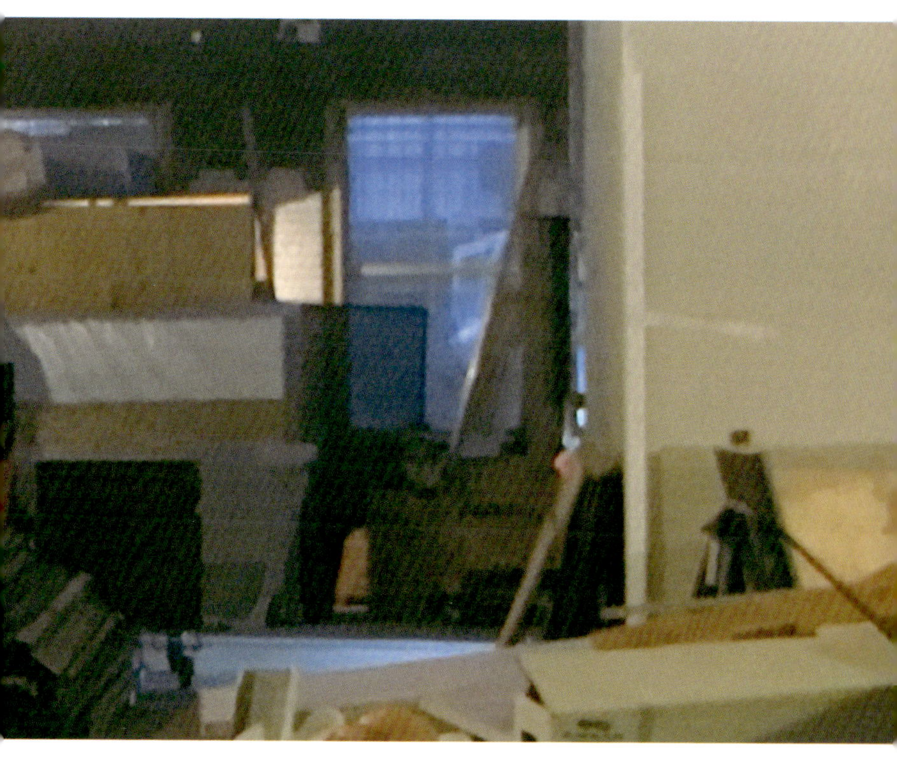